EDUCATION IN A COMPETITIVE AND GLOBALIZING WORLD

ENHANCING K-12 FINANCIAL EDUCATION

A RESOURCE GUIDE FOR POLICYMAKERS

EDUCATION IN A COMPETITIVE AND GLOBALIZING WORLD

Additional books in this series can be found on Nova's website under the Series tab.

Additional e-books in this series can be found on Nova's website under the e-book tab.

EDUCATION IN A COMPETITIVE AND GLOBALIZING WORLD

ENHANCING K-12 FINANCIAL EDUCATION

A RESOURCE GUIDE FOR POLICYMAKERS

LOUIS T. RICHARDSON
EDITOR

nova publishers
New York

Library of Congress Cataloging-in-Publication Data

ISBN: 978-1-63483-139-0

Published by Nova Science Publishers, Inc. † New York

CONTENTS

PREFACE

Integrating financial education throughout the K-12 experience represents a promising opportunity to reach consumers at a pivotal point in their development and their financial lives. This book provides a resource guide meant to help connect policymakers with tools, information, and insights to enhance K-12 financial education efforts. While the guide is targeted at policymakers, the guide was designed to benefit all members of the financial education community. The guide's framework for advancing K-12 financial education has three main sections: laying the groundwork, building the initiative and extending the impact. A second chapter provides an overview of the financial decision-making context that consumers navigate, a review of existing efforts in the K-12 financial education field, and recommendations for advancing financial education in policy and practice.

In: Enhancing K-12 Financial Education ISBN: 978-1-63483-139-0
Editor: Louis T. Richardson

Chapter 1

ADVANCING K-12 FINANCIAL EDUCATION: A GUIDE FOR POLICYMAKERS*

Consumer Financial Protection Bureau

INTRODUCTION

The Consumer Financial Protection Bureau (CFPB) believes integrating financial education throughout the K-12 experience represents a promising opportunity to reach consumers at pivotal points in their development and financial lives. When we start early with age-appropriate and relevant financial education and consistently reinforce those lessons throughout the K-12 years, we can give young people more chances to develop positive habits and behaviors. Helping consumers acquire financial capability is an integral part of the CFPB's consumer financial protection mission, as reflected in numerous provisions of the Dodd-Frank Wall Street Reform and Consumer Protection Act of 2010.[1] The Act charges the Bureau with researching, developing, promoting, and implementing financial literacy programs and activities.

The CFPB developed this resource guide to help connect policymakers with tools, information, and insights to enhance K-12 financial education efforts. The guide will likely be most relevant to state policymakers—notably state treasurers, state superintendents, governors, state legislators, state government associations, and their respective staff—who seek to advance the

* This is an edited, reformatted and augmented version of a document issued April 2015.

development and implementation of K-12 financial education. However, the CFPB designed this resource guide so all members of the financial education community could benefit from the framework, case studies, and resources we have provided. Achieving meaningful and lasting change requires bold and innovative approaches, and involvement of the broad range of stakeholders with a role in implementing financial education.

Embedding financial education within K-12 education can better prepare students for the financial challenges they are likely to encounter in higher education and the workplace. Recent research suggests that, students who receive K-12 financial education achieve significantly higher savings and net worth later in life.[2] Furthermore, carefully implemented high school financial education requirements are linked to improved credit scores and lowered probability of delinquency in young adulthood for students in select states with financial education requirements.[3]

The CFPB aims to support leaders interested in encouraging K-12 financial education by fostering connections among the financial education community and growing the conversation around K-12 financial education initiatives. In 2013, the CFPB furthered these efforts by hosting a national conference on youth financial education and capability and releasing a whitepaper with recommendations for advancing K-12 financial education.

Building upon this foundation, the CFPB set out to better understand the challenges, opportunities, and leading practices for implementing K-12 financial education in school systems throughout the country. We gathered information from a roundtable meeting of K-12 financial education leaders, insights from experts in the field, and further research and analysis. Our work uncovered that while a strong foundation exists to support K-12 financial education, there is a need for greater coordination of efforts and sharing of resources.

How to Use This Guide

Each school system's unique circumstances may require a different combination of approaches to establish and enhance K-12 financial education initiatives. While there are many resources geared at teachers for directly providing K-12 financial education, this guide is designed primarily to help policymakers identify strategies and resources useful for your state. You can start by reviewing the framework and guiding questions on the following pages to identify the specific areas on which you would like to focus.

The subsequent sections of this guide provide case studies of K-12 financial education initiatives from the financial education community. Each case study highlights a specific element of the framework and provides strategies and lessons learned for advancing K-12 financial education. Using the case studies and resources provided, you can extract the ideas and models most applicable to your state's circumstances.

The CFPB does not intend for this policymaker resource guide to be an exhaustive overview of current financial education efforts, nor do we endorse particular initiatives and organizations described in this report. Furthermore, this guide is a working document that CFPB intends to revise and update on an ongoing basis.

For additional information and support or to share your experiences related to advancing K-12 financial education, we encourage you to contact the CFPB at k12financialeducation@cfpb.gov.

FRAMEWORK

The framework set forth in this guide is designed to be simple and intuitive, providing a first step for those just beginning to pursue K-12 financial education or those seeking to enrich existing K-12 financial education initiatives. The framework consists of three sections ("Laying the groundwork," "Building the Initiative" and "Extending the Impact").

Within each module, there are multiple case studies and accompanying resources to illuminate specific efforts needed for advancing K-12 financial education. The CFPB brought together information gathered through an analysis of current efforts, insights shared by K-12 financial education policymakers, as well as discussions with experts and leaders in the financial education community.

Laying the groundwork focuses on making the case for K-12 financial education, setting a strategy for initiatives, defining the structure for initiatives, fostering partnerships, and securing resources.

Building the Initiative focuses on key components of K-12 financial education including standards and requirements, classroom resources, teacher training, and initiative evaluations.

Extending the Impact focuses on implementation, strategies for outreach and recognition, and improving and scaling efforts.

The framework does not constitute a prescription that applies in all situations; unique state circumstances will dictate the specific combinations of approaches that are most applicable. Additionally, CFPB intends to periodically improve and update this policy maker resource guide.

Laying the Groundwork

1.1 Making the case prioritize K-12 financial education and gain buy-in from stakeholders
1.2 Setting the strategy develop the vision and roadmap
1.3 Defining the structure organize people and assets for impact and longevity
1.4 Fostering partnerships engage partners to broaden reach and resources
1.5 Securing resources for K-12 financial launch and sustain the initiative

Building the Initiative

2.1 Standards and requirements set and enforce expectations for learning and instruction
2.2 Teacher training develop capacity for effective financial education delivery
2.3 Classroom resources support dynamic instruction
2.4 Evaluating the initiative assess outcomes and effectiveness

Extending the Impact

3.1 Outreach and recognition motivate communities to own their financial capability
3.2 Improve and scale implement and augment the initiative

GUIDING QUESTIONS

In using this guide, consider the different areas related to K-12 financial education that you may want to initiate, strengthen, or scale, and then review relevant case studies and resources connected to that area. The guide is designed to be flexible and intended to help you advance K-12 financial education.

For each new effort or initiative, consider the high-level framework of laying the groundwork, building the initiative, and extending its impact. Furthermore, as efforts mature, the framework is cyclical providing an opportunity to reassess and align existing efforts. You can then learn and improve strategies and initiatives based on feedback and results from previous initiatives.

To help determine the sections or modules of this guide most relevant to your state needs, consider the following questions. If you answer yes to all the questions in the module, then you may continue to the next set of questions. If you answered no to any question, then are encouraged to review the related module to learn more.

Questions for Advancing K-12 Financial Education

Do state policymakers see K-12 financial education as a priority? Do a wide range of stakeholders and allies currently promote K-12 financial education as a priority? Are specific K-12 financial education initiatives prioritized?	If you answered **no**, then go to **Module 1.1 Making the case**
Is there a strategy within the state government for implementing or enhancing K-12 financial education? Does the strategy include clear choices around where to focus efforts? Does the strategy set measurable goals and objectives for the initiative?	If you answered **no**, then go to **Module 1.2 Setting the strategy**
Is there a clear state government structure in place to implement and enhance K-12 financial education? Does the structure have the longevity and human capital required to realize its stated objectives?	If you answered **no**, then go to **Module 1.3 Defining the structure**
Does your state partner with outside entities (e.g., nonprofit financial institutions, higher education institutions, professional associations) to advance K-12 financial education? Are external partners' capabilities and assets utilized to increase the capacity and reach of K-12 financial education initiatives?	If you answered **no**, then go to **Module 1.4 Fostering partnerships**
Are there existing resources the initiative can draw upon to ensure sustainability? Are there potential sources of funding (consider public-private or public-nonprofit partnerships)?	If you answered **no**, then go to **Module 1.5 Securing resources for K-12 financial education**
Are financial education content standards in place? Is financial education content standards integrated into state testing? Is financial education instruction required?	If you answered **no**, then go to **Module 2.1 Standards and requirements**

(Continued)

Is teacher training on K-12 financial education offered across the state? Does the state government provide incentives and support to encourage teachers to attend training?	If you answered **no**, then go to **Module 2.2 Teacher training**
Are a variety of K-12 financial education resources readily available to teachers and students? Are classroom resources aligned with learning outcomes and state standards?	If you answered **no**, then go to **Module 2.3 Classroom resources**
Are metrics and evaluations in place to determine the success of K-12 financial education initiatives? Are K-12 financial education concepts integrated into assessments?	If you answered **no**, then go to **Module 2.4 Evaluating the initiative**
Do additional opportunities exist for students to engage with K-12 financial education outside of classrooms? Are there clear and consistently communicated messages promoting K-12 financial education? Are there state initiatives in place to recognize advancements in K-12 financial education?	If you answered **no**, then go to **Module 3.1 Outreach and recognition**
Are opportunities available for continuous improvement and the sharing of results? Are structures in place to replicate or scale K-12 financial education initiatives?	If you answered **no**, then go to **Module 3.2 Improve and scale**

1. Laying the Groundwork

The most effective and enduring movements are built on strong foundations. First and foremost, this means building a case and developing a strategic plan to guide further efforts. In addition, this entails ensuring that the right people, systems, partners, and resources are in place to execute on the vision.

The modules that follow in the "Laying the groundwork" section provide examples and resources to initiate and build a strong foundation for K-12 financial education initiatives. The section includes modules describing how to make the case, set a clear strategy, define an organizational structure for the initiative, foster partnerships, and identify potential approaches to secure required resources.

Laying the Groundwork

- **1.1 Making the case** prioritize K-12 financial education and gain buy-in from stakeholders
- **1.2 Setting the strategy** develop the vision and roadmap
- **1.3 Defining the structure** organize people and assets for impact and longevity
- **1.4 Fostering partnerships** engage partners to broaden reach and resources
- **1.5 Securing resources for K-12** financial launch and sustain the initiative

1.1. Making the Case

Policymakers and other stakeholders constantly need to balance numerous competing demands, especially in the education arena. Thus, the first step in advancing K-12 financial education is to establish the case for why K-12 financial education should be a priority.

A strategy for making K-12 financial education a state priority is to make sure the initiative appeals to a wide-ranging base of stakeholders and is backed by data that demonstrates the need for financial education. The following case studies describe some approaches for making the case for K-12 financial education.

Key Questions to Consider in this module:

- Does the case include a variety of inputs to appeal to a range of interests, viewpoints, and supporters?
- Is there evidence-based research and data available to support the case?

Case Studies

New Jersey Summit to Raise Financial Literacy Awareness

In 2010, New Jersey hosted the Financial Literacy: An Imperative for All NJ Students summit to raise awareness of the importance of K-12 financial education across the state. The summit was a result of collaboration between the New Jersey Department of Education, New Jersey Department of Banking and Insurance, the New Jersey Coalition for Financial Education, and Junior Achievement of New Jersey. Participants included policymakers, educators, business leaders, and other key allies to learn about available resources for K-12 financial education and contribute their unique perspectives and viewpoints. The summit supported the newly-adopted state requirement for students to complete a financial, economic, business, and entrepreneurial course for high school graduation.

Source: New Jersey Department of Education
Grades: K-12
Learn more: http:/www.state.nj.us/education

Council for Economic Education (CEE) Survey of the States

The Survey of the States is a twice yearly report that provides a state by state analysis of state policies that have been enacted to require or encourage financial education and economics education instruction in K-12 schools. Specifically, the Survey of the States describes and documents a range of policy options that are available to policy leaders such as high school graduation requirements, creation of content standards, requirements to implement content standards, and student assessment requirements. State leaders in Mississippi have used the results of the survey to draw attention to the need for K-12 financial education.

Source: Council for Economic Education (CEE)
Grades: 9-12
Learn more: http:/www.surveyofthestates.com

Case Study Takeaways

- Initiatives that represent a variety of interests and viewpoints appeal to a range of stakeholders can help to build a broad foundation of support.
- Use research and analysis to help create an impetus for change for K-12 financial education policies.

For additional information please review the *Additional resources laying the groundwork* at the end of this section.

1.2. Setting the Strategy

A good strategy is compelling, actionable, and robust. Strategy that is compelling can generate support from an array of key stakeholders and align a group towards collective impact. In addition, your strategy is actionable if it is easily translated into concrete action plans that are implementable in a relevant timeframe. Finally, a good strategy is robust with tested logic and data to form and validate the choices.

The following case studies provide examples of efforts to set a strategy for K-12 financial education. Every strategy is unique and should be customized to meet the needs of the communities in your state.

Key questions to consider in this module:

- Does the strategy set measurable goals and objectives for the initiative?
- Do these goals address a clear need and tell a compelling story?
- Does the strategy include clear choices around where efforts should focus?
- Do data and insights from a range of stakeholders validate your choices made?
- Does the strategy include direction on how to configure assets and activities to execute upon the objectives?
- Is this strategy actionable and comprehensive?

Case studies

Champlain College Financial Literacy Action Plan

The Center for Financial Literacy at Champlain College in Vermont created a financial literacy task force in response to the state receiving a D grade on the Center's own 2013 *National Report Card on State Efforts to Improve Financial Literacy in High School*. The task force's K-12 committee convened a broad group of policymakers and educators to set a strategy for adopting strong financial education requirements within Vermont. Released at the end of 2014, *Vermont's Financial Literacy Action Plan* provides recommendations for advancing financial capability across K-12 education, higher education, and beyond. The action plan for K-12 financial education emphasizes the need for updating education standards, increasing access to teacher training, and the need for grants to support new efforts. The action plan considers the roles of state policymakers, educators, businesses, and nonprofit organizations to support efforts across the state.

Source: Champlain College
Grades: 9-12
Learn more: http://www.champlain.edu/Documents/Centers-of Excellence/Center-for-Financial-Literacy/VT_FinancialLit_ActionPlan.pdf

Wisconsin Task Force on Financial Education

In 2002, prompted by Wisconsin's low-score on the Jump$tart Coalition's national survey of 12th graders, Wisconsin's governor signed an executive order to establish the task force for financial education with the ultimate goal of improving the financial literacy of Wisconsin's youth. Task force members included representatives of state government, K-12 education, higher education, financial services industry, and nonprofit organizations. The executive order called for the task force to put forth recommendations and set the stage for policy adoption around nine key categories that include: standards and assessment, K-12 courses, partnerships and funding, teacher preparation, incentives, and accountability.

Source: State of Wisconsin
Grades: K-12
Learn more: http:/www.wdfi.org/_resources/indexed/site/ymm/ govcouncilfinlit/final_report.pdf

Mississippi Treasurer's Education about Money Strategy

In 2014, the State Treasury of Mississippi launched a financial literacy initiative called Treasurer's Education About Money (TEAM). TEAM developed a three- year strategy that seeks to provide all high school students in Mississippi access to financial education resources. The initiative also incorporates teacher training through the Mississippi Council on Economic Education.

Source: State Treasury of Mississippi
Grades: 9-12
Learn more: http:/www.treasurerlynnfitch.com/TEAM/Pages/default.aspx

Case Study Takeaways

- Incorporating a range of insights and input can help to ensure the strategy is both robust and compelling, to secure commitment and action from key stakeholders.
- Strategies should include goals and aspirations and outline specific actions for a path forward.
- Goals should be clear and time bound and progress should be measurable.

For additional information please review the *Additional resources laying the groundwork* at the end of this section. Additionally, please review the *Development* tool to set the strategy in the appendix

1.3. Defining the Structure

The success of an initiative depends on the right combination of skills and capabilities, appropriate tools and methods, access to critical stakeholders, and resource allocation. These structural design choices should clearly flow from the objectives and timeframe outlined in a strategy for the initiative.

The following case studies provide examples of state efforts to design a structure for advancing K-12 financial education. Building a structure that transcends administration and leaderships is important for sustaining past efforts. If it is not feasible to house the K-12 financial education initiative within existing government or administrative structures, other potential structures include establishing a council or task force or partnering with outside organizations.

Key questions to consider in this module:

- Does the structure have the longevity and human capital required to achieve objectives?

- Are the right mix of people, skills, expertise and capabilities in place?
- Does the structure include appropriate decision points and processes to make progress and operationalize objectives?

Case Studies

Wisconsin Office of Financial Literacy

Wisconsin's Office of Financial Literacy promotes statewide financial education by operating as an incubator for financial education initiatives. Residing within the Department of Financial Institutions, the Office of Financial Literacy leads and sustains financial education efforts throughout successive administrations. For over a decade, the Office of Financial Literacy develops initiatives and transitions initiatives that are successful to partners. For instance, the office started a three- week teacher training program at a local university. Now, the local university manages and delivers the trainings. The Office of Financial Literacy was created as part of an executive order signed by the Wisconsin governor in 2011.

Source: Wisconsin Department of Financial Institutions
Grades: K-12
Learn more: https:/www.wdfi.org/ymm

Maryland Financial Literacy Education Advisory Council

The Financial Literacy Education Advisory Council supports the state with implementing K-12 financial education standards and the statewide curriculum. The advisory council manages a financial education design team that developed the state's standards and curriculum. The financial education design team comprised of teachers, school administrators, and representatives from financial institutions. The advisory council reports to the State Board of Education on the implementation of K-12 financial education standards and curriculum throughout Maryland.

Source: Maryland State Department of Education
Grades: K-12
Learn more: http://msde.state.md.us/fle/docs/FinancialLiteracy EducationUpdate_112013.pdf

California Legislation Integrating Financial Education into Textbooks

In 2013, California's governor signed into law Assembly Bill No. 166, which called for the state board of education to include financial preparedness topics into social studies, health, and mathematics textbooks and curriculum frameworks when they are revised. This legislation tasked the state board with including topics such as budgeting, managing credit and debt, and student loans for the seventh through the 12th grades. In conjunction with textbook revisions, the state board of education must also develop a financial education curriculum framework.

Source: California Legislature
Grades: K-12
Learn more: http:/www.leginfo.ca.gov/pub/13-14/bill/asm/ab_0151-0200/ab_166_bill_20130826_chaptered.pdf

Case Study Takeaways

- While the specific structure chosen to house an effort may vary, institutionalizing the effort leads to sustainability across administrations resulting in longer lasting impact.
- Clear guidance regarding the individuals or entities responsible can help foster greater accountability for advancing an initiative.

For additional information please review the *Additional resources laying the groundwork* at the end of this section.

1.4. Fostering Partnerships

Strategic partnerships can amplify the impact of K-12 financial education efforts by affiliating individuals and organizations into networks of aligned actors. Potential benefits of fostering partnerships include the ability to collectively solve problems, minimizing duplication, and creating a greater visibility for the issue. By leveraging the capabilities of partners in support of advancing K-12 financial education, impact can extend in a way that is both symbiotic and sustainable.

The first step in fostering partnerships is to identify the goal of the partnership. For example, consider the areas in which partners can build awareness, support implementation, expand influence, and secure funding. Next, identify individuals and organizations with aligned interests and mutually beneficial capabilities in the target region. Also, create an inventory of the organizations and actors currently involved with promoting K-12 financial education. This inventory is likely to include nonprofit organizations, financial institutions, corporations, and higher education as demonstrated in the following case studies.

Key questions to consider in this module:

- Who are potential partners in the financial education community?
- Does the partnership capitalize upon external partners' capabilities and assets to increase the capacity and reach of K-12 financial education initiatives?
- Is the partner relationship symbiotic? Do both sides contribute to each other's objectives?

Case Studies

Financial Education Public-Private Partnership

Established by 2009 legislation in Washington State, the Financial Education Public-Private Partnership (FEPPP) brings together public and private sector members to identify strategies for enhancing K-12 financial education in the state. After identifying strategies, the partnership reviews and recommends financial education resources, provides teacher training, and raises awareness. Additionally, the partnership provides annual reports to state leadership—including the governor, superintendent of public instruction, higher education legislative committee, and K-12 education legislative committee. The partnership includes members across state government, financial institutions, nonprofit, higher education, and professional associations.

Source: Washington State
Grades: K-12
Learn more: http:/feppp.org

Everfi Partnerships

EverFi is a corporation that offers financial education learning platforms for elementary and high school students using new media and technology, including social networking, animations, and gaming. EverFi partners with financial institutions, corporations, and nonprofit organizations to provide its learning platforms to school districts. For example, in Utah, EverFi partners with American Express through the American Express Financial Scholars to bring its program to public schools in San Juan County. Washington Federal partners with EverFi to establish the Washington Federal Financial Scholars program to selected high schools in Arizona, Idaho, Nevada, New Mexico, Oregon, and Utah.

Source: EverFi
Grades: K-12
Learn more: http:/www.everfi.com

State Councils and Centers for Economic Education

The Council for Economic Education (CEE) includes national council, state-level affiliate councils, and centers for economic education located at institutions of higher education. With this localized structure, the CEE network trained more than 55,000 teachers, who ultimately reached 5 million students in 2012. State councils and centers for economic education add capacity and resources to financial education initiatives. State policymakers can benefit from integrating the CEE into their structure to create sustainable efforts for teacher training. In particular, the CEE is equipped to support teachers through local councils and centers for economic education during the adoption of national standards as it did for states including Florida and Mississippi.

Source: Council for Economic Education
Grades: K-12
Learn more: http:/www.councilforeconed.org/resources/local-affiliates

Cooperative Extension, Youth Financial Education

Cooperative Extension is a nationwide educational network that brings research and knowledge of land-grant institutions to people in their homes, workplaces, and communities. The Cooperative Extension links the resources and expertise of more than 3,000 county extension offices, 105 land-grant colleges and universities (which include historically black colleges, tribal colleges, and institutions serving the U.S. territories), and the federal government through USDA's National Institute of Food and Agriculture (NIFA).

Source: USDA's National Institute of Food and Agriculture (NIFA)
Grades: N/A
Learn more: http:/nifa.usda.gov/youth-financial-education

Case Study Takeaways

- Potential partners include leaders from state government, businesses, nonprofit organizations, education institutions, professional associations, and community members.
- Strategic partnerships can both extend the reach of K-12 financial education initiatives, and draw added visibility, resources, and insights to the initiative.

For additional information please review the Additional resources at the end of this section. Additionally, for the *Assessment tool to foster partnerships*, please see the appendix.

1.5. Securing Resources for K-12 Financial Education

The level of resources required for K-12 financial education efforts varies widely, depending on the design, scope, and complexity of the initiative. Regardless, there are many different approaches for obtaining these resources and enhancing the sustainability of financial education efforts. Creative approaches for securing resources have included partnerships with financial institutions, businesses groups, nonprofit organizations, and philanthropies.

The following case studies highlight some approaches for securing resources for K-12 financial education initiatives.

Key questions to consider in this module:

- What existing funding streams are available?
- Is the resource sustainable?
- Can you leverage public-private partnerships to bring vital resources?

Case Studies

New Jersey Legislation for Credit Unions

In 2011, New Jersey's legislature authorized the state's credit unions to take deposits, such as tax receipts, from the state. While serving as public depositories, the credit unions accepting the funds are required to provide funding for K-12 financial education. The legislation authorizes the New Jersey Department of Education, in conjunction with the Department of Banking and Insurance, to select a nonprofit that promotes financial education to receive the funds. The nonprofit receiving the funds is required to provide K-12 financial education.

Source: National Conference of State Legislatures
Grades: K-12
Learn more: http:/www.njleg.state.nj.us/2010/Bills/PL11/108_.HTM

Mayors for Financial Literacy Dollarwise Campaign

DollarWise is a United States Conference of Mayors (USCM) initiative that supports local financial education through its Summer Youth Grants Programs. DollarWise offers the opportunity for USCM members to apply for innovation grants to cities demonstrating financial education commitment to their citizens. Additionally, DollarWise awards grants to cities with innovative efforts to incorporate financial education into their summer youth employment initiatives. DollarWise also promotes financial planning days offering free financial education and planning from certified financial planners. DollarWis*e* has been supported by the Bank of America Foundation since 2005.

Source: United States Conference of Mayors
Grades: K-12
Learn more: http:/bedollarwise.org

State Funding Models

To adequately fund K-12 financial education campaigns, states have employed innovative funding models. West Virginia created a Consumer Education Fund, which receives a percentage of all civil penalties collected by its Division of Banking, to promote consumer awareness and understanding of issues around mortgage lending. Maine uses available funds from the state's unclaimed property fund to help support state K-12 financial education initiatives. Wisconsin uses government settlement funds to develop incentive grants for school districts to implement financial education courses.

Source: Wisconsin's Department of Financial Institutions
Grades: K-12
Learn more: https://www.wdfi.org/newsroom/press/2014/DFI-DPIfinancialLiteracyGrantProgram.pdf

Case Study Takeaways

- Potential strategies include utilizing existing resources or raising outside resources from private sectors organizations, philanthropies, and other bodies committed to K-12 financial education.

For additional information please review the *Additional resources laying the groundwork* at the end of this section.

Additional Resources for Laying the Groundwork

1.1. Making the Case

2013 National Report Card

Collects data from reports and state legislative records to grade every state on its efforts to produce financially literate high school students. Each state is graded based on measures including standalone high school course requirement, assessment of students' financial knowledge, and accountability of financial education implementation requirements.

Source: Champlain College Center for Financial Literacy (CFL)
Grades: 9-12
Learn more: http://www.champlain.edu/Documents/Centers-of-Excellence/Center-for-Financial-Literacy/National-Report-Card-Champlain-College-CFL.pdf

2014 Assets and Opportunity Scorecard

Reviews state by state performance and policy measures across five areas: financial assets & income, business & jobs, housing & homeownership, healthcare and education.

Source: Corporation for Enterprise Development (CFED)
Grades: K-12
Learn more: http:/assetsandopportunity.org/scorecard

Can You Teach Someone to Be Financially Capable? Presentation

Presentation on findings from a meta-analysis of financial education studies and identifies major studies on financial literacy. Includes suggestions on how to set-up a program to provide data that could help better identify cost effectiveness and outcomes.

Source: Organisation for Economic Co-operation and Development (OECD)
Grades: K-12
Source: http://siteresources.worldbank.org/EXTGLOBALFINREPORT/Resources/8816096-1361888425203/9062080-1383688365382/Meta_Analysis_Paper.pdf

Financial Literacy and Education Commission Research Clearinghouse

Contains information on more than 400 reports and articles from federally-supported research, along with a select number of datasets that are available for use in research on financial capability topics.

Source: Mymoney.gov
Grades: K-12
Learn more: http:/www.mymoney.gov/researcher/Pages/for-researchers.aspx

Girl Scouts Research and Advocacy

Research and advocacy to advance financial education opportunities for girls. The Girl Scouts Advocacy Network provides tools for supporting policy initiatives.

Source: Girl Scouts of the USA
Grades: K-12

Learn more: http:/www.girlscouts.org/who_we_are/advocacy/legislative /financial.asp

Investor Education Foundation's National Financial Capability Study

Information on how states compare with other states and the nation on five measures: spending vs. saving, emergency savings, non-bank borrowing, financial literacy, and comparison shopping.

Source: Financial Industry Regulatory Authority (FINR A)
Grades: K-12
Learn more: http:/usfinancialcapability.org

PISA 2012 Results: Students and Money

Examines 15-year old students' performance in financial literacy in 18 countries. Discusses the relationship of financial literacy to students' and their families' background, students' math and reading skills, students' access to money and experience with financial matters.

Source: Programme for International Student Assessment (PISA)
Grades: K-12
Learn more: http:/www.oecd.org/pisa/keyfindings/PISA-2012-results-volume-vi.pdf

State Financial Education Requirements Map

Clickable map allowing user to access financial education requirements by state. Provides details on state laws, curriculum and course requirements. Also provides links to specific state resources.

Source: Jump$tart Coalition
Grades: K-12
Learn more: http:/www.jumpstart.org/state-financial-education-requirements.html

Effectiveness of State Financial Education Mandates

Examines the effectiveness of state mandates on financial education for high school students and documents notable improvements in credit outcomes for young adults who were exposed to rigorous programs.

Source: FINR A Investor Education Foundation

Grades: 9-12

Learn more: http:/www.finra.org/web/groups/foundation/@foundation/documents/foundation/p602380.pdf

Starting Early for Financial Success: Capability Into Action

Journal rigorously explores the connection between financial education and capability interventions, and measurable changes in financial behavior and outcomes.

Source: Journal of Consumer Affairs

Learn more: http:/onlinelibrary.wiley.com/journal/10.1111/(ISSN)1745-6606

1.2. Setting the Strategy

PISA 2012 Assessment and Analytical Framework

Provides a working definition for financial literacy. Content areas described include money and transactions, planning and managing finances, risk and reward and financial landscape. Framework discusses the relationship of financial literacy to non-cognitive skills and math and reading literacy.

Source: Programme for International Student Assessment (PISA)

Grades: K-12

Learn more: http:/www.keepeek.com/Digital-Asset-Management/oecd/education/pisa-2012-assessment-and-analytical-framework/financial-literacy-framework_9789264190511-7-en#page12

Professional Services and Innovation Center

Works to embed financial literacy initiatives into local government infrastructure. Offers technical assistance to city administrations, mayoral candidates, philanthropies and others in developing approaches for financial empowerment at the local level. Provides capacity building to develop and expand upon successful pilot programs, and supports the facilitation of professional development, training, collaboration and fundraising.

Source: Cities for Financial Empowerment Fund

Grades: N/A

Learn more: http:/www.cfefund.org/

Resource Guide

Process-focused resource guide for leaders working to advance financial education in their communities. Guide looks at how to build the case, create a coalition, and drive towards clear outcomes. Includes an appendix of examples of existing programs.

Source: President's Advisory Council on Financial Capability
Grades: K-12
Learn more: http://www.treasury.gov/resource-center/financial-education/Documents/Local%20Guide%20-%20Creating%20Financially%20Capable%20Communities.pdf

Vermont Financial Literacy Summit

Summit convened policymakers, educators, business leaders, and legislators to raise awareness about the need for personal finance education in Vermont.

Source: Champlain College Center for Financial Literacy
Grades: K-12
Learn more: http:/www.champlain.edu/centers-of-excellence/center-for-financial-literacy/cfl-programs/vermont-financial-literacy-summit

Vermont Financial Literacy Task Force

State-wide task force with a goal of making recommendations to Vermont Legislature, educators, employers, and nonprofits around K-12 education, college education, and adults. Task Force is composed of representatives from education, government, business, and nonprofit sector.

Source: Champlain College Center for Financial Literacy
Grades: K-12
Learn more: http:/www.champlain.edu/centers-of-excellence/center-for-financial-literacy/report-vermont-financial-literacy-task-force

State Education Policy Tracker

The ECS tracks state policy trends, translates academic research, provides unbiased advice and creates opportunities for state leaders to learn from one another. Services include State Education Policy Tracking, 50-State Databases and Research Summaries.

Source: Education Commission of the States (ECS)

Learn more: http:/www.ecs.org/default.asp

Building Assets And Building Lives: Financial Capability Programs in Native

Report provides an overview of financial capability programs serving reservation-based Native communities in the Northwest Area Foundation region. The report also discusses promising strategies for increasing financial capability, and provides an environmental scan of successful programs serving Native communities, provides recommendations on how to support financial capability programs, and suggestions for how to most effectively promote these strategies in the region.

Source: First Nation Development Institute

Learn more: http:/www.firstnations.org/knowledge_center/download/building_assets_and_building_lives_financial_capability_programs_native

1.3. Defining the Structure

Bill Tracking AND Analysis

A database of recently introduced or pending state and federal legislation. Includes details about a bill's status and allows users to search by bill text, number, state and author. NCSL provides annual summary of financial literacy legislation and a brief overview of the trends around financial literacy across the country.

Source: National Conference of State Legislatures

Grades: N/A

Learn more: http://www.ncsl.org/research/financial-services-and-commerce/financial-literacy-2014-legislation.aspx

Council On Financial Literacy - Executive Order Establishing Council

Executive Order, signed by Wisconsin's governor on April 6, 2011, establishing Wisconsin's Governor's Council on Financial Literacy.

Source: Governor of Wisconsin

Grades: K-12

Learn more: http://www.wdfi.org/_resources/indexed/site/ymm/govcouncilfinlit/ExecOrder24.pdf

Getting Serious About Financial Literacy: One State's Approach

Overview of the Smart Tennessee program. Program featured public-private partnerships and a teacher training focus.

Source: Journal of Consumer Education

Grades: K-8

Learn more: http:/www.cefe.illinois.edu/JCE/archives/2011_vol_28/2011_vol_28_pg16-24_Heath.pdf

Tennessee Financial Literacy Commission

Structure within the state's Department of Treasury tasked with equipping resident with the ability to make sound financial decisions. Commission that was established through legislation and maintains a clearinghouse of financial resources on its website.

Source: Tennessee Department of Treasury

Grades: N/A

Learn more: http:/treasury.state.tn.us/FinLit/index.html

Financial Literacy Framework

In 2012, Chicago Public Schools integrated new financial literacy coursework into its K-12 curriculum. The Financial Literacy Framework was the result of a partnership with financial leaders from both the private and public sector and provided CPS students with the skills needed to understand finance issues.

Source: Chicago Public Schools (CPS)

Grades: K-12

Learn more: http:/cps.edu/News/Press_releases/Pages/05_10_2012_PR1.aspx

1.4. Fostering Partnerships

CFE Coalition

Convenes municipal governments from across the country that has begun to advance financial empowerment initiatives.

Source: Cities for Financial Empowerment (CFE)
Grades: K-12
Learn more: http:/cfecoalition.org

Delaware's $tand By Me Program

Partnership between the State of Delaware, the United Way of Delaware, and employers to provide a package of financial empowerment services (e.g. one-on-one financial coaching).

Source: State of Delaware
Grades: K-12
Learn more: http:/standbymede.org

Jump$tart State Coalitions

The Jump$tart network consists of 49 affiliated nonprofit state organizations, working as volunteers and ecosystem partners to advance financial education in their respective states

Source: Jump$tart Coalition
Grades: K-12
Learn more: http:/www.jumpstartcoalition.org/state-coalitions.html

Take Charge AZ

Partnership between Take Charge Institute and University of Arizona to build a suite of state and community programs around their national curriculum. Support includes providing university credit for an online personal finance course, training university students as financial educators, and designing the AZ Earn to Learn program providing financial education to high school students.

Source: University of Arizona
Grades: 9-12
Learn more: http:/tcainstitute.org/educProg.html

Financial Football

A game that teaches financial and money management concepts through football. Promoted through partnership with the NFL.

Source: Visa
Grades: K-12
Learn more: http:/www.practicalmoneyskills.com/games/trainingcamp

American Association of Family and Consumer Sciences (AAFCS)

Provides leadership and support to professionals whose work assists individuals, families, and communities in making informed decisions about their well being, relationships, and resources to achieve optimal quality of life. A AFCS is the only professional association for family and consumer sciences (FCS) students and professionals from both multiple practice settings and content areas.

Source: American Association of Family and Consumer Sciences (A AFCS)
Grades: N/A
Learn more: http:/www.aafcs.org

Financial Capabilities Group

Dedicated to empowering New England residents with the knowledge and resources they need to pursue, achieve and sustain their financial wellbeing. Activities include conducting research, engaging practitioners, convening stakeholders and developing online learning tools.

Source: Federal Reserve Bank of Boston
Grades: N/A
Learn more: http:/www.bostonfed.org/index.htm

The ABCs of Credit Finance

State partnered with The Center for Student Credit Card Education to promote a program designed to help high school students learn how to responsibly use a credit card. Program can be downloaded by teachers and students or be taken independently by students online.

Source: State of Iowa
Grades: 9-12
Learn more: http:/www.theabcsofcredit.com

MoneyU

MoneyU offers game-based online courses, and teaches personal finance to young adults.

Source: MoneyU
Grades: K-12
Learn more: https:/www.moneyu.com

1.5. Securing Resources for K-12

Financial Education for College Access and Success Grant

The Department of Education awarded a grant to Tennessee Department of Education. The grant was used to train middle and high school teachers via graduate-level course at Middle Tennessee State University. Course work equals three hours of credit and is fully paid for. Teachers receive a stipend for attending.

Source: U.S. Department of Education
Grades: 6-12
Learn more: http://www.ed.gov/news/press-releases/us-department-education-awards-17-million-tennessee-invest-financial-education-c

Financial Literacy Education Fund

The state of Delaware offers grants to K-12 and adult literacy programs and campaigns related to financial literacy. The available funding comes from an annual licensing fee

Source: Delaware's Office of the State Bank Commissioner
Grades: K-12
Learn more: http:/banking.delaware.gov/services/conedu/flef.shtml

Grant

Grant awarded to Tennessee Financial Literacy Commission to conduct training for elementary and middle school teachers on topics of personal finance.

Source: Dollar General Literacy Foundation
Grades: K-12
Learn more: http:/treasury.state.tn.us/news/PDFs/dollargeneral52813.pdf

National Report Card: Funding Strategies

Section on What Can Be Done and Is Being Done About Funding highlights key funding strategies for financial education efforts within states.

Source: Champlain College Center for Financial Literacy
Grades: K-12
Learn more: https://www.champlain.edu/Documents/Centers-of-Excellence/Center-for-Financial-Literacy/National-Report-Card-Champlain-College-CFL.pdf

2. Building the Initiative

K-12 financial education initiatives should include four primary interconnected parts, all working in concert: educational content standards and requirements, teacher training, high quality classroom resources, and rigorous initiative evaluation. While we understand that each state has unique circumstances when it comes to financial education implementation, content standards and requirements can help set expectations about the knowledge and skills students must demonstrate. Trained teachers can skillfully deliver as well as adapt the curriculum in ways that are developmentally appropriate and engaging to students. High-quality classroom instructional materials help actualize the standards. Lastly, rigorous evaluation methods help measure the impact and effectiveness of the instruction, allowing you to continuously monitor and improve components of the initiative.

The modules that follow contain information to support the design and implementation for each of these components—standards and requirements, teacher training, classroom resources, and evaluation—to build robust and scalable K-12 financial education initiatives.

Building the Initiative

- **2.1 Standards and requirements** set and enforce expectations for learning and instruction
- **2.2 Teacher training** develop capacity for effective financial education delivery
- **2.3 Classroom resources** support dynamic instruction
- **2.4 Evaluating the initiative** assess outcomes and effectiveness

2.1. Standards and Requirements

Education standards outline expectations about the knowledge, concepts, and skills that students should acquire at each grade level and are a crucial reference point for designing and evaluating K-12 financial education initiatives. While 43 states now include financial education in their curriculum standards, many stop short of requiring schools to implement those standards. When the law does not require implementation of K-12 financial education standards, they are voluntary and schools are less likely to adopt them. Standards and requirements are needed to both implement and scale K-12 financial education. The case studies below provide insight into some of the standards available and options for bringing standards to the classroom.

Key questions to consider in this module:

- What K-12 financial education content standards are in place? How do they vary by grade level?
- Are financial education standards tied to an existing course or required to be taught as part of a stand-alone course?
- Do state tests include K-12 financial education standards?
- How do you enforce standards? Do associated requirements exist around the standards (e.g., is financial education a graduation requirement)?

2.1.1. Content Standards

When seeking to adopt content standards, review existing state standards, then review national standards developed by financial education organizations. Two of the leading national standards include the Council for Economic Education's (CEE) K-12 National Standards for Financial Literacy and the

Jump$tart Coalition's National Standards in K-12 Personal Finance Education. These standards define the knowledge and skills that students must master at each level. Moreover, the standards make it easier to evaluate student financial knowledge and determine outcomes and effectiveness. While there are nuances to the two sets of standards, both encourage financial education with a focus on the fourth, eighth, and 12th grades.

Case Studies

Colorado Department of Education Review of Potential Standards

In an effort to determine the best strategy for implementing K-12 financial education standards, the Colorado Department of Education (CDE) considered four options for incorporating standards. These included embedding K-12 financial education standards within both social studies and mathematics; within either mathematics or social studies; adopting national standards and aligning to math, English language arts, and/or social studies standards; or developing state-specific, customized standards. CDE considered the states employing the approaches, specifics around how the approaches looks in practice, and the appropriateness of the approaches to Colorado's specific needs. Ultimately, Colorado integrated personal finance standards into its K-12 social studies and mathematics standards.

Source: Colorado Department of Education's
Grades: K-12
Learn more: http:/www.cde.state.co.us/standardsandinstruction /pflreview

Jump$Tart Coalition's National Standards in K-12 Personal Finance Education

Jump$tart's National Standards delineate the personal financial knowledge and ability that young people should acquire throughout K-12 school years. The standards focus on six key topic areas: spending and saving, credit and debt, employment and income, investing, risk management and insurance, and financial decision-making. Jump$tart developed the standards with support from partners in business, finance, government, academia, education and other key stakeholders.

Source: Jump$tart Coalition
Grades: K-12
Learn more: http:/www.jumpstartcoalition.org/national-standards.html

The Council for Economic Education (CEE) National Standards for Financial Literacy

The National Standards for Financial Literacy provides a framework for teaching personal finance from kindergarten to 12th grade. The standards focus on six key topics: earning income, buying goods and services, using credit, saving, financial investing, and protecting and insuring. In 2014, Florida was the first state to adopt CEE's updated standards. Florida financial education policymakers chose to include the standards as a part of the Next Generation Sunshine State Standards (NGSSS) for Social Studies. The standards appear as a distinct strand, on par with economics, geography, world history, and other key topics, within the NGSSS for grades four, eight, nine and 12. The standards underpin the new Economics with Financial Literacy course graduation requirement for students entering ninth grade during the 2013-2014 academic years. Florida's chapter of the CEE hosts workshops to support teachers in their implementation of the new requirements.

Source: Council for Economic Education
Grades: K-12
Learn more: http:/www.councilforeconed.org/resource/national-standards-for- financial-literacy

2.1.2. Implementation Requirements

State governments can take several approaches for requiring K-12 financial education standards and for implementing those standards in the classroom. These include explicitly mandating that high school students complete a stand- alone course in personal finance, as in Virginia, Utah, Tennessee, and Missouri. Alternatively, states may require school districts to include K-12 financial education as part of another course—such as family and consumer sciences, economics, mathematics, or social studies— as do Georgia, Idaho and Louisiana.

Case Studies

Missouri K-12 Financial Education Requirements

In 2002, Missouri's governor signed an executive order calling for recommendations to advance K-12 financial education which was informed through the efforts of the Missouri Council on Economic Education, the Missouri Bankers Association, and the Missouri State Treasurer. With no pre-existing standards or requirements for K-12 financial education, the report included recommendations for teacher preparation, funding initiatives, graduation requirements, and necessary legislation changes required to improve K-12 financial education. Based on the 2014 results of the Council of Economic Education's (CEE) Survey of the States, Missouri is one of three states, along with Georgia and Texas, to have all of the CEE recommended requirements for financial education. Missouri adopted K-12 financial education standards, requires districts to implement K-12 finance standards, requires high school students to take a personal finance course, and requires standardized testing to include finance topics.

Source: State of Missouri
Grades: K-12
Learn more: http:/www.sos.mo.gov/library/reference/orders/2002/eo02_008.asp

Case Study Takeaways

- Decisions regarding the most appropriate set of standards to adopt vary based on specific needs of the state.
- If the state does not require schools to implement financial education standards, schools are significantly less likely to teach financial education because of competing requirements.

For additional information please review the *Additional resources for building the initiative* at the end of this section.

2.2. Teacher Training

While a number of states have adopted financial education standards, only 11 percent of teachers attended a financial education workshop within the past three years, according to a 2009 National Endowment for Financial Education survey. Moreover, over 60 percent of teachers said they "don't feel qualified" to teach financial education. Effective teacher professional development is essential to prepare educators for teaching K-12 financial education that meet state standards and requirements in the classroom.

Key questions to consider in this module:

- What opportunities exist for teachers to gain familiarity and skill in teaching K-12 financial education?
- Who provides incentives and support to encourage teachers to attend trainings?

The following case studies serve as examples of existing teacher training programs, including summits, conferences, and summer institutes. Regardless of the format, strong professional development programs should focus on ensuring that teachers feel comfortable with the content and can access resources they can easily implement in their classrooms.

Case Studies

The Jump$Tart Teacher Training Alliance (J$TTA)

J$TTA is a collaborative endeavor designed to standardize teacher training in personal finance thorough a shared model called Jump$tart Financial Foundations. The J$TTA is administered by the Jump$tart Coalition on behalf of its partners and affiliates. Founding members of J$TTA include Council for Economic Education, Jump$tart Coalition, Junior Achievement USA, National Endowment for Financial Education, and the Take Charge America Institute at the University of Arizona. The model is available at no cost to qualified users and is designed to complement existing teacher training programs.

Source: Jump$tart Coalition

Grades: N/A

Learn more: http:/www.jumpstartcoalition.org/teacher-training-alliance.html

The Jump$Tart Educator Conference

Each year, the Jump$tart Coalition hosts a National Educator Conference geared toward Pre-K-12 educators. The conference provides participants with resources, professional development, and networking opportunities between educators and financial professionals. Additionally, Jump$tart's state coalitions host Educator Conferences focused on honing educators' skills, providing access to up-to-date curricula and tools, and networking with colleagues.

Source: Jump$tart Coalition

Grades: K-12

Learn more: http:/www.jumpstartcoalition.org/teacher-conference.html

Wisconsin's Office of Financial Literacy National Institute of Financial and Economic Literacy

Wisconsin's Office of Financial Literacy, in partnership with the Wisconsin Jump$tart Coalition and Edgewood College, offers three courses each summer. Designed for teachers, the coursework focuses on incorporating K-12 financial education concepts in personal finance, family and consumer sciences, social studies, economics, math, and business courses. The Office of Financial Literacy encourages financial counselors, technical college faculty, corrections staff, and school principals and administrators to attend.

Source: Edgewood College

Grades: K-12

Learn more: http:/www.edgewood.edu/Events/NIFEL

Click, Learn, and Teach

Click, Learn, and Teach is a series of free online professional development programs on K-12 economics and financial education from the Federal Reserve Banks of Atlanta and St. Louis. Teachers can earn Graduate Credit, Federal Reserve Bank Certification, or Continuing Professional Development Units in certain states.

Source: Federal Reserve Banks of Atlanta and St. Louis
Grades: K-12
Learn more: https:/www.stlouisfed.org/education/teacher-professional-development

Tennessee Financial Literacy Summits

The Tennessee Department of Treasury's Financial Literacy Commission, a nonprofit organization created by the Tennessee General Assembly, conducts a series of free summits on financial education for K-8 teachers throughout the state. The sessions are designed to increase teacher comfort with financial education curriculum, and include financial advisors allowing teachers to ask questions about their retirement planning options. The summits count toward a teacher's continuing education credits and sometimes provide other incentives to encourage participation. More than 1,800 teachers from across the state received the training in a two-year period.

Source: Tennessee Department of Treasury
Grades: K-8
Learn more: http:/www.proedtn.org/?TNFLCsummits2014

Champlain College Summer Institute

Champlain College designed a one-week professional development program to increase the financial education and instructional capability of Vermont's K-12 teachers. The program uses a curriculum compiled by a national steering committee that includes the Jump$tart Coalition, the National Endowment for Financial Education, the Council for Economic Education, Federal Deposit Insurance Corporation , Family Economics and Financial Education, Junior Achievement, the U.S. Department of Education, and U.S Department of the Treasury.

Source: Champlain College Center for Financial Literacy
Grades: 9-12
Learn more: http:/www.champlain.edu/centers-of-excellence/center-for-financial-literacy/cfl-programs/vermont-teachers-financial-literacy-summer-institute

Case Study Takeaways

- Offering flexible platforms for participation, such as trainings during the summer or online courses, can help address teachers' time constraints during the school year.
- Providing incentives for participation, such as continuing education credits or other incentives can help encourage attendance.
- Whether the program leverages existing curriculum or uses proprietary materials, the most successful teacher training programs work to ensure teachers feel comfortable with the material at hand and are well prepared to implement it in their classrooms.

For additional information please review the *Additional resources for building the initiative* at the end of this section.

2.3. Classroom Resources

Many resources already exist to support the delivery of K-12 financial education initiatives, reducing the need to create new classroom resources. Though local decision makers often select classroom resources, state-level leaders can support the process. Policymakers may consider age-appropriate initiatives that align with the expectations of school districts and the state. Furthermore, students are more likely to learn from financial education materials if they are relevant to students' lives. The following includes examples of resource repositories, K-12 financial education curricula, and supplemental programs and materials.

Key questions to consider in this module:

- Are resources readily available to teachers and students?
- Do classroom resources fully align with learning outcomes or state standards?
- Do classroom resources present a variety of rich educational content at relevant and appropriate points for students?
- Are the resources objective and balanced?
- Do classroom resources integrate easily with existing standards and curricula?

2.3.1. Resource Repositories

A collection of classroom lesson plans and activities are available in various clearinghouses and repositories. While these provide helpful starting points for building a K-12 financial education initiative, it is important to provide selection and choice for educators while also ensuring that resources are age-appropriate, relevant and, most importantly, effective.

Case Studies

UTAH Finance in the Classroom

Finance in the Classroom is a repository of K-12 financial education resources managed by Utah's State Office of Education (USOE) and the Utah Education Network (UEN). Resources available on this website include standards, curricula, lessons, books, videos, and more. Furthermore, USOE worked with educators to design a matrix that assigns financial and economic concepts to grade levels. By providing ideas for integrating age-appropriate financial content into existing courses, such as mathematics, social studies, and language arts, Finance in the Classroom makes it easy for teachers to introduce K-12 financial education concepts early and reinforce them consistently throughout the K-12 school years.

Source: Utah Department of Education/ Utah Education Network
Grades: K-12
Learn more: http:/financeintheclassroom.org

The Jump$Tart Clearinghouse

The Jump$tart Clearinghouse is an online library of financial education resources geared toward educators and parents. Jump$tart staff review submissions to the Clearinghouse against criteria aligned to Jump$tart's national standards. The Clearinghouse includes more than 800 resources for use in and outside the classroom for kindergarten through college. Each resource includes a description, associated cost, appropriate grade level, target user, resource type, and a link to the resource's website.

Source: Jump$tart Coalition
Grades: K-12
Learn more: http:/www.jumpstartcoalition.org/jump$tart-clearinghouse.html

MyMoney.gov

MyMoney.gov is a repository that provides financial education resources developed by federal government agencies of the Financial Literacy and Education Commission (FLEC). The website includes resources on the five principles that consumers have in mind as they make day-to-day decisions, and plan their financial goals (*My Money Five*). In addition, there are resources such as budget work sheets and money quizzes. FLEC is a federal commission comprised of 21 federal entities, including the White House Domestic Policy Council and is chaired by the Treasury Department and vice chaired by the CFPB. The purpose of the FLEC is to coordinate and collaborate to strengthen financial capability and increase access to financial services for all Americans.

Source: FLEC
Grades: K-12
Learn more: http:/www.mymoney.gov/Pages/default.aspx

The Federal Deposit Insurance Corporation (FDIC) Money Smart

The FDIC developed *Money Smart* as a comprehensive financial education curriculum designed to help low- and moderate-income individuals outside the financial mainstream enhance their financial skills and create positive banking relationships. *Money Smart* has several instructor-led modules for specific communities, including

Money Smart for Adults, Money Smart for Youth, and Money Smart for Older Adults.

Source: FDIC
Grades: K-12
Learn more: https:/www.fdic.gov/consumers/consumer/moneysmart/ young.html

Federal Reserve Education

The website, FederalReserveEducation.org, provides free resources designed to help teachers and educators teach personal finance, economics, and related topics. The website is created and hosted by the Federal Reserve Board and provides a range of lesson plans, multimedia, games and simulations for teaching topics such as financial education, economics, and monetary policy.

Source: Federal Reserve
Grades: K-12
Learn more: http:/www.federalreserveeducation.org

Sesame Street for Me, for You, for Later

This online, bilingual resource is targeted towards kindergarteners. It includes videos, printable activity books, and educator guides focused on making good financial choices, the value of money, and spending, sharing, and saving.

Source: Sesame Street
Grades: K-2
Learn more: http:/www.sesamestreet.org/parents/topicsandactivities/toolkits/save

2.3.2. Curricula

K-12 financial education curricula and classroom resources should align to appropriate content standards, be easy to implement in the classroom, and allow teachers to differentiate instruction based on the needs of the student. Below we provide some examples of K-12 financial education curricula and classroom resources.

Case Studies

National Endowment for Financial Education (NEFE) High School Financial Planning Program

High School Financial Planning Program (HSFPP) provides financial concepts and skills focused on basic financial education concepts relevant to pre-teens, teens, and young adults. The program contains six module topics (planning, borrowing, earning capability, investing, financial services, and insurance), and includes six student guides, an assortment of 45-minute teacher lesson plans, and a collection of online resources and learning activities.

Source: National Endowment for Financial Education
Grades: 9-12
Learn more: http:/www.hsfpp.org

Council For Economic Education (CEE) Financial Fitness for Life

Financial Fitness for Life is an economic and financial education program for students in grades K-12. Topics covered in the curriculum include earning and income, consumer decision-making and spending, saving and investing, money management, and using credit wisely. The curriculum consists of teacher guides, student workbooks, and parent guides that correspond to different grade levels, and interactive games and activities. In Nevada, for example, the Treasurer's office sent the curriculum to every middle and high school in the state, and coordinated several classroom pilots utilizing the curriculum.

Source: Council for Economic Education (CEE)
Grades: K-12
Learn more: http:/fffl.ncee.net

Take Charge Today

The University of Arizona's Take Charge America Institute offers *Take Charge Today* a program and curriculum with a decision-based approach to personal finance. The *Take Charge Today* program is founded on the idea that a university- based financial education outreach program can strengthen and extend the ability of schools and community organizations to improve the personal financial capabilities of young adults. Content lesson plans are available at the introductory (targeted at grades 7-9) and advanced (targeted at grades 10-12) levels.

Source: University of Arizona
Grades: 6-12
Learn more: http:/tcainstitute.org/takechargetoday.html

Money As You Learn

Money as You Learn is an initiative of a coalition of nonprofit organizations, teachers, academics, and other experts seeking to implement the President's Advisory Council on Financial Capability's recommendations regarding strengthening the financial literacy of the nation's young people. Money as You Learn offers educators tools to integrate personal finance into the teaching of the Common Core State Standards in Mathematics and English Language Arts, as well as into other classes and after-school programs. In addition, Money as You Grow has been developed as parallel initiative to target parents and kids. Money as You Grow offers 20 essential, age-appropriate financial lessons—with corresponding activities.

Source: President's Advisory Council on Financial Capability
Grades: K-12
Learn more: http://www.moneyasyoulearn.org
Learn more: http://www.treasury.gov/resource-center/financial-education/Documents/Money%20as%20You%20Grow.pdf

My Money, My Future

My Money, My Future is an online program that provides a financial education course that aligns with Virginia's high school state standards for financial education. The program supports students and teachers with the state's one credit economics and personal finance graduation requirement. Over 75% of Virginia high schools use the program.

Source: Genworth Foundation
Grades: K-12
Learn more: https://www.genworth.com/corporate/about-genworth/in-the-community/my-money-my-future.html

2.3.3. Supplemental Programs and Materials

Supplemental programs and materials that can be used in the classroom and beyond provide additional opportunities for experiential learning. Experiential learning opportunities give students the opportunity to practice, reflect, and learn. This can be achieved through activities that emphasize role-play, simulations, and group work. For example, initiatives that pair financial education with savings accounts at schools, special goal-based child savings accounts with built-in incentives, and game-based learning all have elements of experiential learning.

Case Studies

Finance Park

Finance Park is a Junior Achievement program designed for middle and high school students that includes several weeks of lessons, online games and activities, and a one-day field trip to the local Junior Achievement chapter. The Finance *Park*, offers students the chance to take part in reality-based decision-concerning key aspects of personal finance such as family budgeting, investing, philanthropy, and banking. The program also includes a series of classroom follow-up activities occurring over the course of two weeks.

Source: Junior Achievement USA
Grades: 6-8
Learn more: http:/www.myja.org/financepark

National Credit Union Foundation Financial Reality Fair

Financial Reality Fairs give students an opportunity to experience financial decision-making in a simulated setting. Students choose a career and practice budgeting and money management.

Source: National Credit Union Foundation
Grades: K-12
Learn more: https:/www.ncuf.coop/how-we-help/real-solutions/experiential/reality-fairs.cmsx

Awesome Island Game

Awesome Island Game is a finance education game that was created by financial education experts and teachers to gamify learning. The game provides an interactive way for students to learn the basics of budgeting, saving, taxes, debt, careers and income, philanthropy, and investing. The game takes two hours to complete and to serves as an opening activity for a unit on financial education.

Source: Champlain College
Grades: 3-8
Learn more: http:/www.awesomeislandgame.com

My Classroom Economy

Created by Vanguard and 5th grade teacher, My Classroom Economy is a classroom economic system that teaches financial education through simulation. Students earn school "dollars" through classroom jobs and pay rent for desks, pay fines for breaking classroom rules, and make purchases. The program is customizable by grade level and is designed to overlay classroom curriculum that aligns to the Common Core State Standards.

Source: Vanguard
Grades: K-12
Learn more: http:/myclassroomeconomy.org

Bank at School Programs

Across the country, several partnerships are in place to offer access to savings accounts to students. These programs often provide experiential learning opportunities to students by allowing them a chance to manage a savings account and practice saving toward future goals. Pilot studies of bank at school programs in Eau Claire, Wisconsin, and Amarillo, Texas, demonstrated student knowledge gains in financial literacy, positive increases in students' perceptions of banking and saving, and significant increases in the likelihood of having a bank account as an adult.

Source: Royal Credit Union
Grades: K-5
Learn more: http:/www.rcu.org/investments_and_savings/school _sense.phtml

Online and Mobile Gaming Programs

Many organizations have been developing interactive tools and games to reach young people through technology. For example, Mind Blown Labs has created Thrive 'n' Shine, an experiential financial capability application where players earn money, which has to be strategically saved and spent throughout the course of the game. Players learn lessons about budgeting, saving, credit score management, and debt management through the interactive game. Doorways to Dreams (D2D) has administered hackathons and competitions to spur the development of mobile applications that improve financial access and capability for underserved consumers, jointly administered with the Center for Financial Services Innovation (CFSI). These include the FinCapDev Competition and MyMoneyAppUp Challenge. Money Think designed Moneythink Mobile, an interactive social platform designed to enable mentors to issue their mentees challenges that build financial awareness, habits, and skills. Through the app, students are rewarded with points and social affirmation (in the form of digital likes and comments) as they complete challenges.

Source: Money Think
Learn more: http:/moneythink.org/our-program/our-approach

Source: Mind Blown Labs
Learn more: http:/www.mindblownlabs.com/product
Source: D2D
Grades: N/A
Learn more: http:/www.d2dfund.org/mobile_apps

Case Study Takeaways

- States have a wide variety of resources to choose from when building out their K-12 financial education initiatives.
- Regardless of the instructional materials designed or approved, classroom resources should align to state standards and expectations, and be developmentally appropriate.

For additional information please review the *Additional resources for building the initiative* at the end of this section.

2.4. Evaluating the Initiative

As with any new effort, it is critical to establish milestones, benchmarks, and metrics to assess outcomes and measure progress. Methods of measuring the success of K-12 financial education efforts include using metrics such as rubrics and student assessments, as well as evaluating broader K-12 financial education progress through standardized testing.

Key questions to consider in this module:

- How do you define success for your initiative?
- Do standardized assessments include K-12 financial education concepts?

2.4.1. Initiative Assessment

While no one universal method of evaluating the quality and effectiveness of K-12 financial education initiatives exists, there are a number of assessment banks and toolkits available for identifying and incorporating appropriate evaluation mechanisms. These resources include:

Case Studies

National Endowment for Financial Education (NEFE) Evaluation Toolkit

NEFE's Evaluation Toolkit supports K-12 financial educators and nonprofits in understanding concepts around evaluation and applying those concepts to educational programs. The toolkit consists of two main parts: an evaluation manual with guidance on how to design appropriate evaluation methods, and impact indicators for programs. Evaluations allow educators and funders to determine the impact of a particular program and identify and address the areas in need of improvement. The toolkit includes a database with evaluation templates and allows educators to save completed evaluations to their account.

Source: National Endowment for Financial Education (NEFE)
Grades: K-12
Learn more: http:/toolkit.nefe.org

The Council for Economic Education (CEE) Online Assessment Center

CEE's Online Assessment Center (OAC) is a free service that allows teachers to securely administer assessments, gain real-time data, and measure student knowledge of economic and personal finance concepts. The service allows teachers to analyze the effectiveness of their instruction and adjust accordingly. The OAC offers teachers the ability to analyze individual and class data by test and test item. Teachers can track individual student and class wide programs, evaluate student performance compared to standards and benchmarks, and develop custom reports of student and class performance. Assessments are available for upper elementary school, middle and high school, and university levels.

Source: Council for Economic Education (CEE)
Grades: K-12
Learn more: http:/www.councilforeconed.org/resource/online-assessment-center

Georgia Milestones Assessment System Economics, Business, and Free Enterprise Assessment

The Georgia Milestones Assessment System, administered by the state's Department of Education, requires students to take end-of-course assessments in a variety of subjects. Milestones measure student achievement and provide feedback to teachers, districts, and the state about their instructional practice and program delivery. For high school students, an assessment serves as a final course exam and the score counts as 20 percent of a student's final grade in the appropriate course. The system includes an assessment on economics, business, and free enterprise, of which 20 percent covers financial education topics, including saving, credit, insurance, and income. The assessment includes both criterion-referenced (aligned to state-adopted content standards) and norm-referenced (yielding national comparison) items, allowing for multiple evaluation opportunities.

Source: Georgia Department of Education
Grades: 9-12
Learn more: http://www.gadoe.org/Curriculum-Instruction-and-Assessment/Assessment/Documents/GM%20Economics%20EOC%20Assessment%20Guide.pdf

Case Study Takeaways

- The design and delivery of K-12 financial education should include evaluation metrics.
- Standardized evaluation measures allow for more accurate program comparisons across regions, thus creating opportunities for sharing of promising practices and potentially identifying areas for improvement.

For additional information please review the *Additional resources for building the initiative* at the end of this section.

Additional Resources for Building the Initiative

2.1.1. Content Standards

ABA/CFED Road to Financial Responsibility

Infographic that helps parents or educators identify concepts and content most appropriate for students at a given age.

Source: American Bankers Association/ Corporation for Enterprise Development (ABA/CFED)

Grades: K-12

Learn more: http:/www.aba.com/Engagement/Documents/TCTS-14-Tips%20sheet-FINAL.pdf

Common Core Alignment Tool

Aligns lessons from select resources to the Common Core State Standards; searchable by resource or by standard.

Source: Center for Economic Education

Grades: K-12

Learn more: http:/www.councilforeconed.org/resource/common-core-state-standards/

Model Academic Standards for Personal Financial Literacy

Statewide financial literacy content standards covering knowledge and skills, across all grade levels and disciplines. Designed for educators to align instruction and create curriculum and activities toward financial literacy and sound financial habits.

Source: Wisconsin's Department of Public Instruction

Grades: K-12

Learn more: http:/standards.dpi.wi.gov/sites/default/files/imce/standards/pdf/pfl.pdf

National Standards for Business Education – Personal Finance

National standards, including focus on personal finance.

Source: National Business Education Association's

Grades: K-12

Learn more: http:/www.nbea.org/newsite/curriculum/standards/index.html

National Standards for Family and Consumer Sciences Education

National standards, including focus on personal finance.

Source: National Association of State Administrators of Family and Consumer Sciences

Grades: K-12

Learn more: http:/www.nasafacs.org/national-standards-and-competencies.html

2.1.2. Implementation Requirements

State Financial Education Requirements Map

Interactive map detailing the personal finance requirements state by state, including relevant legislation and curriculum.

Source: Jump$tart Coalition

Grades: K-12

Learn more: http:/www.jumpstartcoalition.org/state-financial-education-requirements.html

2.2. Teacher Training

Strengthening Financial Education in California (Working Paper)

An analysis of possible strategies for implementing statewide financial education in California. Provides a review of the national and state approaches and recommends a specific set of steps for California, including enhancing teacher preparation and incentivizing school districts.

Source: Federal Reserve Bank of San Francisco

Grades: K-12

Learn more: http:/www.frbsf.org/community-development/files/wp 2010-02.pdf

2.3.1. Resource Repositories

Financial Literacy Database

Includes resources for teaching economics and money management, including translated articles, interactive calculators, lesson plans, videos and quizzes.

Source: Rosen Digital

Grades: 6-12

Learn more: http:/financialliteracy.rosendigital.com

2.3.2. Curricula

Money Smart

A financial education curriculum available in different versions: CD-ROM, self-paced computer based instruction and podcast. Curriculum is available for Young Adults (ages 12-20) and Elementary School Students (ages 5-8), and consists of customizable modules, which can be taught on a stand-alone basis.

Source: Federal Deposit Insurance Corporation
Grades: K-12
Learn more: https:/www.fdic.gov/consumers/consumer/moneysmart

Financial Literacy Initiatives Presentation

Provides an overview of financial education initiatives in Nevada, including Financial Fitness for Life. Provides data on and provides recommendations to enhance state-wide initiatives.

Source: Nevada State Treasurer
Grades: K-12
Learn more: http://www.treasury.gov/resource-center/financial-education/Documents/Marshall%20presentation.pdf

EverFi Financial Literacy, Vault

Learning platform that uses technology—video, animations, 3-D gaming, avatars, and social networking—to provide financial education. The platform offers students simulations of real- life experiences, provides assessment data, and awards badges and certifications for successful completion. Available for elementary and high school students.

Source: EverFi
Grades: 3-12
Learn more: http:/www.everfi.com/vault

2.3.3. Supplemental Programs and Materials

Biz Kid$

Award winning TV show to teach teens about personal finance. The show spans five seasons and the website provides activity guides, lesson plans, games, and a teacher discussion forum. Content is aligned national standards for financial literacy and entrepreneurship education.

Source: PBS
Grades: 9-12
Learn more: http:/bizkids.com

Delaware Bank at School Program

Provides banking opportunities to students in schools. Teachers are encouraged to teach financial education in classrooms to reinforce lessons.

Source: Delaware Financial Literacy Institute
Grades: K-5
Learn more: http:/www.bankatschool.com/history.html

Gen I Revolution

Provides fifteen missions in which students complete a variety of activities to help them learn important personal finance concepts. Within each mission, students are introduced to a character that is facing a particular financial crisis. As a part of the Gen i Revolution, the student learns about the crisis, strategically selects "Operatives," and then completes activities with the ultimate goal of solving the mission.

Source: Council for Economic Education (CEE)
Grades: 9-12
Learn more: http:/www.genirevolution.org

Goventure Personal Finance Card Game

Card-based educational game with activities includes question-and-answer, drawing, charades, trivia, and word puzzles. Supported by a suite of free resources including a GoVenture "cheat sheet" glossary and educational standards alignment.

Source: MediaSpark, Inc.
Grades: 6-12
Learn more: http:/www.goventure.net/Products/PFCG/Summary.aspx

Green$treet Commons

Video based gaming apps for children, ages 5-8.

Source: Green$treet Commons

Grades: K-2

Learn more: http:/greenstreetcommons.com

Keys to Financial Success

A 54-lesson course plan for teaching personal finance, available at no cost to schools and teachers. Incorporates free professional development. Course aligns with the Council for Economic Education and Jump$tart national standards.

Source: Federal Reserve Bank of Philadelphia

Grades: 9-12

Learn more: http:/www.philadelphiafed.org/education/teachers/resources/keys-to-financial-success

Khan Academy, Bank of America 'Better Money Habits'

Series of videos around personal finance issues, such as credit scores, managing debt and home buying. Participants earn points for viewing videos and quiz performance.

Source: Khan Academy Bank of America

Grades: 9-12

Learn more: https:/www.bettermoneyhabits.com/index.html

Kindergarten to College (K2C)

K2C is the City of San Francisco's initiative to provide every student entering Kindergarten in the City's public schools with a College Savings Account (CSA) containing a $50 deposit from the City and County of San Francisco. Account is used as a teaching tool for financial education.

Source: San Francisco Office of Financial Empowerment

Grades: K-2

Learn more: http:/sfofe.org/programs/k-to-c

Money As You Learn

Provides teachers with lesson plans that are aligned to the Common Core State Standards for Math and English language arts. Classroom resources are available for grades K-2, 3-5, 6-8, and 9-12.

Source: President's Advisory Council on Financial Capability
Grades: K-12
Learn more: http:/www.moneyasyoulearn.org

Practical Money Skills Games

Game based lessons for financial education that connect to a series of age-specific lesson plans. Games include Financial Soccer, Financial Football, Money Metropolis, and Peter Pig's Money Calculator. Designed for classroom and at-home use.

Source: Visa, Inc.
Grades: 3-8
Learn more: http:/www.practicalmoneyskills.com/games

Money Habitudes

Interactive activity centered on a deck of cards which describes a range of money attitudes, engaging learners in self-identification and group discussion. Helps place personal finance topics in the context of the student's life, which makes later lessons more relevant.

Source: Lifewise Strategies, LLC
Grades: 6-12
Learn more: http:/www.moneyhabitudes.com/user-types/teachers-youth-leaders

High School Financial Planning Program

Program focused on basic personal finance skills for pre-teens, teens, and young adults. Program is organized into six topic-based modules with student guides, an assortment of 45-minute teacher lesson plans, and a collection of online learning activities.

Source: National Endowment for Financial Education (NEFE)
Grades: 9-12
Learn more: http:/www.hsfpp.org

Financial Education and Account Access among Elementary Students Research Brief

Findings of a research study commissioned by the US Department of the Treasury about the impact of in-school bank branches on elementary school students' financial knowledge. Findings describe the role of financial education and account access on improving student knowledge and attitudes.

Source: Corporation for Enterprise Development (CFED)
Grades: K-5
Learn more: http:/cfed.org/assets/pdfs/AFCO_youth_brief.pdf

The Stock Market Game

The Stock Market Game program is an online simulation of the global capital markets that engages students in grades 4-12 in the world of economics, investing and personal finance.

Source: SIFMA Foundation
Grades: 4-12
Learn more: http:/www.stockmarketgame.org/index.html

MyCreditUnion.gov

MyCreditUnion.gov offers information on how to start a student run credit union at school and also provides addition financial tools and resources.

Source: National Credit Union Association
Grades: K-12
Learn more: http:/www.mycreditunion.gov/Pages/credit-unions-in-schools.aspx

My Financial Guide

Wells Fargo offers various resources on financial education, including calculators, student planning, and information on budgeting and managing credit.

Source: Wells Fargo
Grades: N/A
Learn more: https:/www.wellsfargo.com/financial-education

Schwab Money Wise

The website provides information on money basics, calculators, and resources for parents and educators.

Source: Charles Schwab
Grades: N/A
Learn more: http:/www.schwabmoneywise.com/public/moneywise/about/financial_literacy

2.4.1. Initiative Assessment

Money F-I-T

White paper focused on need to and structure of near-term and long-term assessments of students' financial literacy.

Source: Center for Financial Security, University of Wisconsin-Madison
Grades: 3-5
Learn more: http:/moneyfitevaluation.wordpress.com

Planning Curriculum in Personal Financial Literacy

Comprehensive guide on developing curriculum around personal financial literacy which aligns with Wisconsin's Model Academic Standards for Personal Financial Literacy. Includes strategies for building a program, planning instruction, creating assessment, and designing professional development. Includes sample activities and rubrics.

Source: Wisconsin's Department of Public Instruction
Grades: K-12
Learn more: http:/finance.dpi.wi.gov

Youth Savings Pilot

FDIC to collect data from financial institutions currently offering youth savings programs and support the development of new programs. For participants, FDIC will help foster networking, offer workshops on new resources, troubleshoot implementation issues, and provide technical assistance. Participating institutions must apply to the FDIC.

Source: Federal Deposit Insurance Corporation (FDIC)
Grades: K-12

Learn more: https:/www.fdic.gov/consumers/banking/youthsavingspilot

Research Priorities & Research Questions

Priorities are used to inform FLEC, other government agencies, academic researchers on important questions facing the field.

Source: Financial Literacy Education Commission (FLEC)
Grades: K-12
Learn more: http://www.treasury.gov/resource-center/financial-education/Documents/2012%20Research%20Priorities%20-%20May%2012.pdf

3. EXTENDING THE IMPACT

Stagnant initiatives run the risk of becoming obsolete. Even if an initiative utilizes the best strategies and resources, it will not realize its intended impact without a consistent focus on ongoing outreach and enhancement. To create, capture, and sustain value, it is critical to extend the reach of K-12 financial education initiatives by engaging a broad community of stakeholders, and by building a framework to measure, adapt, and strengthen initiatives over time.

The following section contains guidance on how to effectively carry out and augment K-12 financial initiatives, including resources to support the promotion and recognition of efforts, and improve and scale existing initiatives.

Building Extending the Impact

3.1 **Outreach and recognition** motivate communities to own their financial capability
3.2 **Improve and scale** implement and augment the initiative

3.1. Outreach and Recognition

Engaging external stakeholders through awareness and outreach is an important complement to any K-12 financial education initiative. The objective of these efforts is to amplify conversations and recognize successful K-12 financial education efforts to drive a broader base of support.

Key questions to consider in this module:

- What is your engagement strategy?
- Do the channels align to your target stakeholders and constituents?
- Do you communicate messages clearly and consistently? Who provides recognition for successful efforts?

As demonstrated in the examples below, outreach efforts may include social media, competitions, or events.

Case Studies

Missouri's #Finlitfriday Initiative

Using social media and the hashtag #FinLitFriday, Missouri promotes financial education among Missourians. The initiative shares financial education resources and money management tips around budgeting, building credit, and investing. The #FinLitFriday campaign provides studies and advice from financial experts including the Federal Reserve and U.S. Treasury Department.

Source: Missouri State Treasurer
Grades: 9-12
Learn more: http://www.treasurer.mo.gov/newsroom/news-and-events/item/2014/07/31/treasurer-zweifel-announces-new-social-media-campaign-to-enhance-financial-literacy-among-missourians

National Financial Literacy Month

April is National Financial Literacy Month which highlights the importance of financial literacy and aims to teach Americans how to establish and maintain healthy financial habits. In 2000, the National Endowment for Financial Education introduced Youth Financial Literacy Day. In 2003, the United States Senate designated April as Financial Literacy for Youth Month. In March 2004 the Senate passed Resolution 316 that officially recognized April as National Financial Literacy Month. Every year the President issues a proclamation to recognize the month.

Source: The White House
Grades: K-12
Learn more: http:/www.whitehouse.gov/the-press-office/2014/03/31/ presidential-proclamation-national-financial-capability-month-2014

Minnesota Department of Commerce Financial Capability Month

Minnesota's Governor proclaimed April 2014 as the state's Financial Capability Month – in line with the President's National Financial Capability Month. Throughout April, ten state agencies conducted nearly 40 educational and outreach events promoting financial education. The month provides several events specifically targeted to parents of students. To draw attention to the opportunity to use children's literature to teach K-12 financial education, the state's Commerce and Education Commissioners conducted a joint event celebrating the *It's Never too Early to Start* parent's and teacher's guide.

Source: Minnesota Department of Commerce
Grades: K-12
Learn more: http://mn.gov/commerce/consumers/financial-literacy /financial-capability-month.jsp

Lights, Camera, Save! Contest

The American Bankers Association (ABA) *Lights, Camera, Save!* video contest engages teenagers in educating themselves, sharing their knowledge, and building awareness of financial education. For the 2014-2015 school year, the grand prize winners of the video contest receive a cash prize and a scholarship for a teacher from their school to attend Jump$tart's National Educator Conference. The contest involves local banks to host early rounds of the contest and select a winner to compete nationally.

Source: American Bankers Association (ABA)
Grades: 6-12
Learn more: http:/www.aba.com/Engagement/pages/lcsinfo.aspx

America Saves Week

Started in 2007, America Saves Week is a national initiative involving more than 1,000 nonprofit, government, and corporate groups that encourages individuals and families to save money and build personal wealth. America Saves and the American Savings Education Council coordinate the annual event, and the Consumer Federation of America (CFA) provides overall management for the initiative.

Source: America Saves
Grades: K-12
Learn more: http:/www.americasavesweek.org/home-2

Money Smart Week

Created by the Federal Reserve Bank of Chicago in 2002, the annual Money Smart Week public awareness campaign focuses on promoting financial literacy and stronger personal financial management. The campaign includes the support of businesses, financial institutions, schools, nonprofits, government agencies, and the media. Topics covered during the week include budgeting, credit, home buying, and retirement planning. Events throughout the United States appear on the Money Smart Week website. Schools can take advantage of the events and resources provided by Money Smart Week to introduce or focus on K-12 financial education.

Source: Federal Reserve Bank of Chicago
Grades: K-12
Learn more: http:/www.moneysmartweek.org

Case Study Takeaways

- Platforms for successful outreach initiatives include social media, competitions, and events.
- State initiatives can build upon a number of existing public awareness campaigns, such as Money Smart Week, National Financial Capability Month, and America Saves Week.
- Outreach efforts should encompass a variety of constituents, including parents, students, and teachers and recognize successful K-12 financial education efforts.

For additional information please review the *Additional resources for extending the impact* at the end of this section.

3.2. Improve and Scale

After building the initiative, it is essential to ensure strategies are in place to improve and scale the initiative. Given the considerable work still to be done in the field of K-12 financial education, there is a need for continuous efforts to increase rigor and enhance evaluation methods.

Key questions to consider in this module:

- Are structures in place for identifying areas for continued improvement?
- What mechanisms are in place to share results and add to the body of knowledge of what works?

As seen in the following examples, feedback mechanisms such as surveys, pilots, and studies can serve as useful tools to identify areas for further improvement. Regardless of the path chosen, it is important for state policymakers and the financial education community to share findings and add to the growing body of collective information and experiences.

Case Studies

Maryland State Department of Education (MSDE) Implementation of Personal Financial Literacy Education

Since 2011, Maryland has required all school systems to offer financial education for students in grades 3-12. The MSDE implemented K-12 financial education as part of its efforts to promote college and career readiness. Overseen by an advisory council, a financial literacy education team developed statewide standards and curriculum with supporting indicators and objectives. Following acceptance by the State Board of Education, local schools implemented requirements to adopt a financial education program at the elementary, middle, and high school levels. Beginning a five-year cycle of re-approval, the MSDE required all local superintendents to submit their school system's approach to implementing the state standards and curriculum to the state superintendent. During this process, the MSDE provided implementation support, including funding, monitoring, and evaluation of local implementation efforts. Additionally, MSDE monitors ongoing state needs through surveys to identify areas of improvement. Following the rollout of the requirements, MSDE administered a survey asking school systems to describe the delivery of financial education at the various grade levels and what additional resources were still needed to assist with this initiative. Based on teacher survey responses, MSDE plans to expand teacher training 0pportunities by developing teacher toolkits and an online teacher course for financial education.

Source: Maryland State Department of Education (MSDE)
Grades: K-12
Learn more: http://msde.state.md.us/fle/docs/FinancialLiteracy EducationUpdate_112013.pdf

Vermont High School Pilot Study

The state of Vermont partnered with Champlain College's Center for Financial Literacy to study the effectiveness of highly trained teachers on financial education outcomes in Vermont high schools. The state has financial education standards and requirements, but wanted to understand what else was required to develop successful financial education programs in its schools. The initiative will also identify the best practices of the teachers involved in the pilot through the creation of a *Professional Learning Community* of educators which will be funded by the pilot program. These teachers will share their results and recommendations to all their teachers at the completion of this program via a website delivery mechanism. Businesses and private donors provided much of the financial support for the study.

Source: Champlain College Center for Financial Literacy
Grades: 8-12
Learn more: http://www.champlain.edu/centers-of-excellence/center-for-financial-literacy/cfl-programs/high-school-pilot-program

Case Study Takeaways

- Conduct research (e.g., surveys or focus groups) to identify and prioritize areas of need.
- Set clear objectives and indicators to define and measure impact on an ongoing basis.

- Work to address areas for improvement and growth in a strategic and sustainable manner.

For additional information please review the *Additional resources for extending the impact* at the end of this section.

ADDITIONAL RESOURCES FOR EXTENDING THE IMPACT

3.1. Outreach and Recognition

Life Smart

Competition for students in 6-12th grade. Participants focus on five areas: consumer rights and responsibilities, the environment, health and safety, personal finance, and technology.

Source: National Consumers League
Grades: 6-12
Learn more: http:/lifesmarts.org

Merit Badges

Credentials around financial literacy, throughout the progression from Daisy to Ambassador, are offered. Topics include: budgeting, financing and comparison shopping.

Source: Girl Scouts of the USA
Grades: 3-12
Learn more: http:/www.girlscouts.org/research/publications /financial_ literacy

Personal Management Merit Badge

Credential, necessary to achieve the rank of Eagle Scout focuses on financial literacy and time management skills. Requirements to obtain the badge include preparing a budget, writing a plan for purchasing a large item and demonstrating knowledge and understanding around personal finance.

Source: Boy Scouts of America
Grades: 6-12

Learn more: http://www.scouting.org/scoutsource/BoyScouts/AdvancementandAwards/MeritBadges/mb-PERM.aspx

Financial Literacy Award

PWC's Financial Literacy Award recognizes educators who are helping their students develop responsible financial behavior by prioritizing financial literacy curricula.

Source: PWC
Grades: 9-12
Learn more: http://www.pwc.com/us/en/about-us/corporate-responsibility/commitment-to-youth-education/financial-literacy-award.jhtml

3.2. Improve and Scale

The Gallup-Hope Index

Index to measure youth attitudes about entrepreneurship and financial literacy, gain insight into how they envision their economic future, and understand their level of participation in our nation's economy. Research is paired with strategies and intervention to advance financial education.

Source: Operation HOPE
Grades: K-12
Learn more: http:/www.operationhope.org/Gallup-HOPE-Index

Make Your Path (My Path)

Initiative providing disadvantaged youth with peer-led financial capability trainings, a savings account at a mainstream financial institution and incentives to set and meet savings goals. Program focuses on youth earning their first paycheck, which is a critical moment to promote savings and connect youth with financial products.

Source: Federal Reserve Bank of San Francisco
Grades: 9-12
Learn more: http:/cfed.org/assets/pdfs/MY_Path_Working_Paper_2013-03.pdf

OECD Tools to Measure Financial Literacy and Identify Core Competencies

Overview of three tools developed by OECD: 1) financial literacy survey to capture levels of financial literacy in adults; 2) financial literacy assessment developed as part of PISA; 3) core competency framework for youth, which draws on the findings of the PISA 2012 financial literacy assessment.

Source: Organisation for Economic Cooperation and Development (OECD)

Grades: K-12

Learn more: http:/www.esma.europa.eu/system/files/7_adele_atkinson_oecd.pdf

State Mandated Financial Education and the Credit Behavior of Young Adults

Illustrates utilizing credit report data as an example of how to evaluate the efficacy of financial education interventions.

Source: Federal Reserve Board

Grades: K-12

Learn more: http:/papers.ssrn.com/sol3/papers.cfm?abstract_id =2495884

U.S. Bank-Fullerton Partnership

Highlights the partnership of California State University-Fullerton with U.S. Bank to provide financial education training for middle and high school teachers and to create a Youth IDA program for low- and moderate-income students. The IDA program will also underpin a longitudinal study of the impact of Youth Individual Development Accounts over a five-year period.

Source: U.S. Bank and California State University-Fullerton

Grades: 6-12

Learn more: http:/financialgenius.usbank.com/about

Pathways to Progress

In partnership with the Cities for Financial Empowerment Fund, the Citi Foundation increased their commitment to Summer Jobs Connect, which provides low income youth with summer work experience, access to financial education, and financial services.

Source: Citi Foundation
Grades: 9-12
Learn more: http:/www.citigroup.com/citi/news/2015/150303b.htm

NEXT STEPS

There is an exciting opportunity to design and implement policies and practices to help develop the financial capability of young people to make financial decisions and manage their money over their lifetimes.

The CFPB recognizes the value in raising awareness of K-12 financial education, supporting K-12 financial education research and program evaluation, and acknowledging successful K-12 financial education initiatives and practices. In doing so, the CFPB supports policymakers in advancing K-12 financial education as it best suits each state, locality, and classroom.

This guide is a starting point for discussions that build awareness of and interest in what is possible for K-12 financial education. The framework, case studies, and resources in this guide point to approaches for building the capability to develop sustainable and impactful initiatives. The CFPB plans to update this guide on an ongoing basis to include new and innovative approaches to K-12 financial education.

The CFPB encourages you to use and share this guide to advance K-12 financial education. For more information on the information in this guide, or to share your experiences, best practices, or resources, please contact the CFPB at k12financialeducation@cfpb.gov.

APPENDIX A: CFPB RESOURCES FOR ADVANCING K-12 FINANCIAL EDUCATION

In addition to this guide, the CFPB provides a variety of resources to promote K-12 financial education. The list of resources below indicates the name of the resource source, a brief description, and web link.

2014 Financial Literacy Annual Report

Outlines the Bureau's strategy to improve financial literacy, and highlights from past and ongoing initiatives.

http:/files.consumerfinance.gov/f/201407_cfpb_report_financial-literacy-annual-report.pdf

Corresponding Module: Fostering partnerships

Transforming the Financial Lives of a Generation of Young Americans: Policy Recommendations for Advancing K-12 Financial Education

Provides an overview of the financial decision-making context that consumers navigate a review of existing efforts in the K-12 financial education field, and recommendations for advancing financial education in policy and practice.

http:/files.consumerfinance.gov/f/201304_cfpb_OFE-Policy-White-Paper-Final.pdf

Corresponding Module: Making the case, Setting the strategy

Investing in Our Future: National Conference on Youth Financial Education & Capability

Discussion summary of the April 2013 conference hosted by CFPB, which centered on defining a collective vision for the field, promising practices for including financial education in K-12 schools, the role of innovative, hands-on learning, and research and evaluation needs.

http:/files.consumerfinance.gov/f/201312_cfpb_summary_youth-financial-capability-conference.pdf

Corresponding Module: Setting the strategy, Defining the structure

Community Partnership Guidebook for Libraries

Toolkit for libraries to utilize when developing partnerships to support financial education programming. Includes planning worksheets and replicable forms.

http:/files.consumerfinance.gov/f/201406_cfpb_partner-guidebook.pdf

Corresponding Module: Fostering partnerships, Define the Structure, Improve and scale

Paying for College

Web-based 'action guide' including tools designed to inform and support students as they navigate college financial aid and student debt.

http:/www.consumerfinance.gov/paying-for-college

Corresponding Module: Classroom resources

Your Money, Your Goals

Toolkit for social services organizations, designed to support goal-setting and developing personal financial management skills for their clients.

http:/www.consumerfinance.gov/your-money-your-goals

Corresponding Module: Setting the strategy, Fostering partnerships, Improve and scale

Financial Well-Being: the Goal of Financial Education

This report provides a conceptual framework for defining and measuring success in financial education by delivering a proposed definition of financial well-being, and insight into the factors that contribute to it.

http:/www.consumerfinance.gov/reports/financial-well-being

Corresponding Module: Making the case, Evaluating the initiative

Building Financial Capability in Youth Employment Programs

This report provides an overview of lessons learned during a roundtable that the CFPB convened in collaboration with other federal agencies to discuss integrating financial education into youth programs, establishing partnerships with employers, and identifying effective strategies to collaborate with financial institutions.

http:/www.consumerfinance.gov/reports/building-financial-capability-in-youth-employment-programs

Corresponding Module: Making the case

Ask CFPB

Online tool, which provides answers to over 1,000 questions about financial products and services. It answers questions on topics including mortgages, credit cards, and how to fix an error in a credit report.

http:/www.consumerfinance.gov/askcfpb

Corresponding Module: Classroom resources

CFPB Brochures

The CFPB created a range of publications for consumers that provide straightforward information about money management and other financial issues. These publications include brochures about checking your credit report, avoiding checking account fees, tax-time saving, how to avoid foreclosure, what to do if you cannot pay your credit card bills, and other topics. The CFPB makes many of these resources available in both English and Spanish. These publications are available for free download or bulk order.

http:/promotions.usa.gov/cfpbpubs.html

Corresponding Module: Classroom resources

CFPB/FDIC Parents and Caregivers Initiative

The CFPB is collaborating with the Federal Deposit Insurance Corporation (FDIC) on an initiative to empower American youth to make better financial decisions to achieve their own goals throughout the stages of their lives. The collaboration focuses on improving youth financial capability by developing and promoting financial education resources for youth, parents and caregivers of youth, and teachers. The collaboration will build on the FDIC's Money Smart financial education program to address youth from preschool through age 20, and will also develop resources for parents and teachers.

http:/www.consumerfinance.gov/parents

Corresponding Module: Outreach and recognition, Improve and scale

Financial Aid Shopping Sheet

The Financial Aid Shopping Sheet is a standardized, easy-to-read form of financial aid award letter that colleges and universities can send to prospective students. The Shopping Sheet is designed to allow college applicants to better understand the debt implications of their college choice and compare the costs and financial aid offers of the schools from different institutions. http:/www.consumerfinance.gov/students/knowbeforeyouowe

Corresponding Module: Classroom resources, Improve and scale

APPENDIX B: DEVELOPMENT TEMPLATE TO SET THE STRATEGY

Setting the strategy is a key component of laying the groundwork for K-12 financial education efforts. After making the case for financial education and generating support from the appropriate stakeholders, it is critical to develop a sound strategy for the initiative. This strategy will form the foundation for the initiative's design and execution, guiding resource allocation, performance measurement, and ongoing decision making and adaptation.

The strategy development tool that follows outlines the primary elements to consider when setting the strategy for an initiative. It is designed as a starting point for surfacing an initial strategic concept that will then feed into the development of a comprehensive strategy and plan, but should not be used as the sole input into a finalized overarching strategy.

Components of an Effective Strategy

In order to turn vision into impact, effective strategies align choices in four key areas: identifying goals and objectives, focusing efforts, outlining activities, and identifying the assets and capabilities required. These choices should be integrated and mutually reinforcing, such that each choice supports those preceding and following it (e.g., capabilities and systems identified should support the aspirations for the initiative).

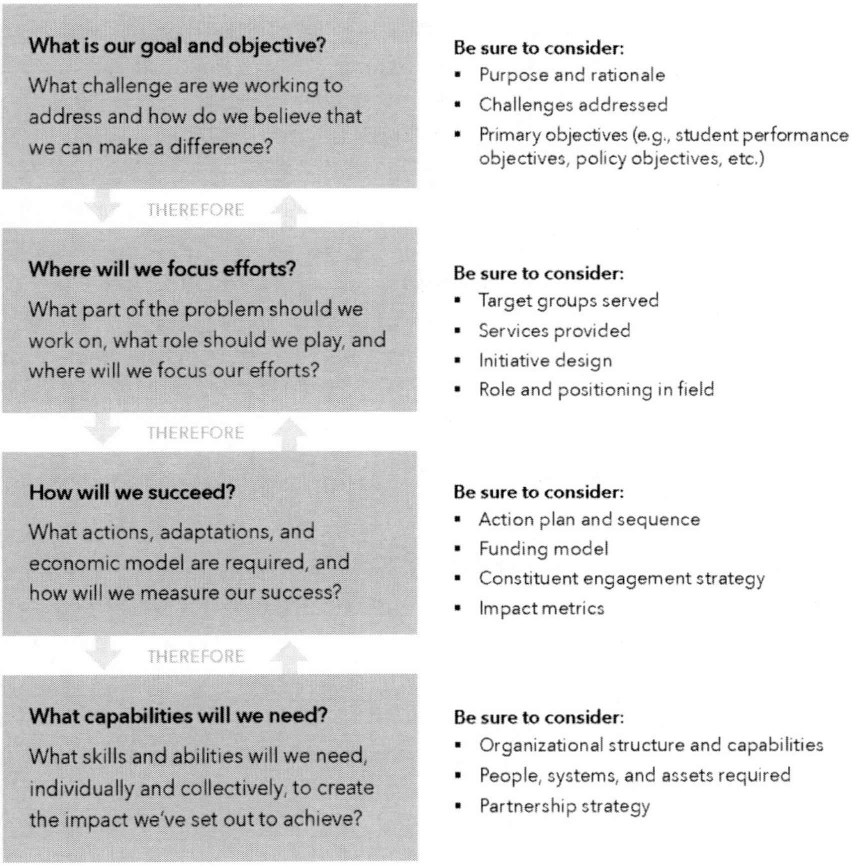

Figure 1. Components of an Effective Strategy.

- **What is our goal and objective?:** This includes defining the purpose and rationale for the initiative, challenges it will address, and primary objectives. The best goals are measurable, time-bound, ambitious yet attainable, and address a clear need.
- **Where will we focus efforts?:** This includes who you seek to impact, what services you will provide, the program design to deliver them, and the role and positioning for the initiative in the field. These choices will not only guide where to direct your efforts, but also where not to focus, which helps to ensure that time and resources are used efficiently.

- **How will we succeed?:** A strategy is only useful if a clear path exists to drive its implementation, including an action plan and sequence, funding model, constituent engagement strategy, and impact metrics. Once a clear goal and focus has been identified, the action plan and sequence lays out the necessary activities to achieve short and long term impact. The resources and constituent engagement strategy help sustain the work, while impact metrics measure the value of these activities and progress towards your goal.
- **What capabilities will we need?**: In order to effectively execute upon your aspirations, the goals and focus of the initiative must be well-supported by aligned systems and resources. These include an organizational structure outlining the people, systems, and assets required to deliver the work, along with a partnership strategy to fill in any gaps in resources or capabilities.

The best strategies are compelling to a range of stakeholders, actionable and realistic given the capabilities and resources available, and logically sound and coherent. These three characteristics – compelling, actionable, and robust – should guide the design of the strategy, as well as pressure test the strategy to confirm its strength.

In order to generate a strong foundation of support for the initiative, the strategy needs to be compelling and purposeful, to ensure the commitment of key stakeholders, both cognitively and emotionally. In addition, it should be actionable and attainable, able to be translatable into concrete action plans with realistic timelines supported by the requisite capabilities and resources.

Please see an illustrative example of how this tool might be used to generate initial thoughts around setting the strategy for an initiative. In addition, a template and guiding questions for thinking through the key initial considerations when setting your K-12 financial education strategy is included following the illustrative example.

What is our goal and objective?

Primary objectives:
- Develop highly trained mathematics teachers that are committed and capable of effectively integrating personal finance concepts in their general classroom instruction

Challenges addressed:
- Educators' discomfort with teaching personal finance topics
- Limited instructional time available for personal finance education

Impact targets:
- Train 100 teachers across the state annually
- Expose 700 classrooms to personal finance education which has been integrated into existing mathematics instruction by 2018

Where will we focus efforts?

Target groups:
- 9-12th grade math teachers across the state

Services provided:
- Training on use of personal finance for math educators curriculum and resources
- One-on-one financial planning consultations for participants

Program model:
- Week long summer training institute

Role and positioning:
- While several teacher trainings and conferences related to personal finance are offered throughout the year, this will serve as the only intensive summer institute targeted specifically towards math educators in the state

How will we succeed?

Action plan:
- Training design and development will run from January - May
- The training will be held in mid-June

Constituent engagement:
- Offer continuing education credit and other incentives to teachers for their participation
- Reach out to principals and superintendents to encourage their teachers to attend

Economic model:
- Leverage higher education partners and philanthropic donors to defray the costs of the initiative

Impact metrics:
- Number of teachers trained
- Teacher satisfaction survey results
- Implementation rates in mathematics classrooms

What capabilities will we need?

Organizational structure:
- The program will be designed and led by the Office of Financial Literacy
- A task force will be responsible for the Institute's development period; once the training is operational ongoing management will be led by the Office's Chief of Staff

Capabilities required:
- Experienced instructors
- Space to hold trainings and board participants
- Strong outreach capabilities to attract participants

Partnership strategy:
- Partner with local college for space, Jump$tart for curriculum, and district leaders to encourage their teachers to attend

Figure 2. An Illustrative Example.

What is our goal and objective?

- What is our primary organizational goal/ objective?
- What is the specific challenge we are looking to overcome?
- What impact are we seeking to have?

Primary objectives:

____

____

____

Challenges addressed:

____

____

____

Impact targets:

____

____

____

Where will we focus efforts?

- What groups of people do we want to impact?
- What services will be provided?
- What program design will deliver them?
- What unique role will the initiative serve in the field?

Target groups:

____

____

Services provided:

____

____

____

Program model:

____

____

Role and positioning:

____

____

____

Figure 3. Strategy Development Template (Part 1).

How will we succeed?

- What key activities are required, and how do we sequence them to meet our short and long-term goals?
- How will we measure the value we provide?
- Who are our primary stakeholders, and how will they be involved?
- What is a sustainable economic model for the short and long term?

Action plan:

____

____

____

Constituent engagement:

____

____

____

Economic model:

____

____

Impact metrics:

____

____

____

____

What capabilities will we need?

- What kinds of people, systems, and assets are required?
- What organizational and governance structure will be most effective?
- What partnerships will we need to have with other individuals and organizations?

Organizational structure:

____

____

____

____

Capabilities required:

____

____

____

____

____

Partnership strategy:

____

____

____

Figure 3. Strategy Development Template (Part 2).

Strategy Development Template

The example below provides an illustration of employing the strategy development tool outlined above. This example sets an initial strategic concept for a hypothetical teaching training initiative. The CFPB does not intend this to be an endorsement of any specific approach, but rather is included for demonstrative purposes only.

The template below serves as a starting point for surfacing an initial strategic concept or thought starter, rather than a comprehensive strategy. Before finalizing a strategy, it is important to incorporate the appropriate stakeholders for a vetting process.

APPENDIX C : EVALUATION TEMPLATE TO FOSTER PARTNERSHIPS

Efforts to foster partnerships are an essential element to lay the groundwork for financial education. After defining an internal structure for the initiative, policymakers can expand the impact and scope of your efforts through tapping into outside resources and support. These partnerships can bring added skills, resources, and insight into the initiative's design and implementation.

The following steps outline the primary factors to consider when fostering partnerships. The CFPB designed this template as a starting point to identify and assess high potential relationships. This is not intended to act as a comprehensive partnership strategy and plan.

Steps for Identifying Partnerships

First, evaluate the current landscape for K-12 financial education in your region. To do this, conduct an inventory of the organizations, programs, and individuals in your area already involved with financial education initiatives. These may include government and community leaders, financial institutions, financial education experts, nonprofit organizations, libraries, and other community service providers, academic or research institution businesses.

Next, assess the potential benefits the partnership. Partners can bring a variety of capabilities and perspectives to the table, including:

- Knowledge and data of what works
- Influence and ability to effect change within the education infrastructure
- Added visibility and awareness to the issue
- Business and financial acumen
- Financial and professional resources
- Practical insights on the issues and concerns of community members

In addition, successful partnerships are reciprocal, so it is important to consider the potential partner's motivations for the relationship. For example, through working with state government offices, potential partners stand to gain added visibility and recognition. In addition, partnerships formed at the local level can then be scaled across states if the partnership proves successful. Taken together, hypotheses around the "give" and "get" can offer a greater sense of the potential value and feasibility of the relationship. Based on these measures, you should work to prioritize the highest-value feasible partnerships.

Finally, turn intention into action by thinking through the best avenues for establishing the prioritized partnerships and appropriate contacts for initiating the relationship.

Partnership Evaluation Template

The template below provides a starting point to think through the partnership development process, from cataloging the various organizations in your area to beginning the relationship. The row below of the template provides a few examples for you to consider. The CFPB does not intend this template as an endorsement of any specific approach or a comprehensive partnership assessment or strategy, but rather is included for demonstrative purposes only.

Table 1. An Illustrative Example

Organization or Program	Type	Potential Partnership Value ("Give")	Incentives for Partner ("Get")	Recommended Approach
Organization X	Local nonprofit, bank or credit union, academic institution, etc.	Knowledge and research, influence and ability to effect change, visibility and awareness, etc.	Alignment with organization's purpose, marketing value, etc.	One-on-one meeting with Program Director, email with attached infographic to Corporate Social Responsibility lead, etc.

Table 2. Partnership Evaluation Template

Organization or Program	Type	Potential Partnership Value ("Give")	Incentives for Partner ("Get ")	Recommended Approach

End Notes

[1] An important financial literacy mandate is set forth in Section 1013(d) of the Dodd-Frank Act, which directs the Bureau, through its Office of Financial Education, to develop and implement initiatives intended to "educate and empower consumers to make better informed financial decisions" and to "develop and implement a strategy to improve the financial literacy of consumers." (12 U.S.C. § 5493(d)(1) &(2)). The Dodd-Frank Act also mandated the creation of other offices within the Bureau that are responsible for, among other things, developing financial education and policy initiatives to support the financial well-being of particular segments of the consumer population (12 U.S.C. § 5493(b), (e), (g)).

[2] United States Department of the Treasury, "Integrating Financial Education into School Curricula." (2002)

[3] FINR A Investor Education Foundation, "State Financial Education Mandates: It's All in the Implementation." (2015)

In: Enhancing K-12 Financial Education ISBN: 978-1-63483-139-0
Editor: Louis T. Richardson

Chapter 2

TRANSFORMING THE FINANCIAL LIVES OF A GENERATION OF YOUNG AMERICANS: POLICY RECOMMENDATIONS FOR ADVANCING K-12 FINANCIAL EDUCATION[*]

Consumer Financial Protection Bureau

MESSAGE FROM RICHARD CORDRAY DIRECTOR OF THE CFPB

When America was confronted with the worst financial crisis since the Great Depression, many families felt helpless in the face of joblessness, falling home prices, the rising cost of higher education, and diminished savings. Many were shaken in their deeply held belief that they could work hard, behave responsibly, and get ahead in life. As the American economy recovers, we want consumers to be able to look ahead with renewed hope and resilience.

The Consumer Financial Protection Bureau (CFPB) is working toward an improved marketplace by providing effective rules, consistent oversight, and evenhanded enforcement. Moreover, we seek to ensure that product marketing and disclosures are transparent, so individuals may compare products and make informed decisions. And we want consumers of all ages to have the opportunities and resources to improve their financial capability so they are

[*] This is an edited, reformatted and augmented version of a document issued April 2013.

able to navigate the financial marketplace effectively and take more control over their economic lives.

During my years in state and local government, I became deeply engaged in consumer finance issues. I saw good people struggling with debt they could not afford. Sometimes they made bad decisions they came to regret. Sometimes an unexpected event – like a loved one getting sick or a family member losing a job – overwhelmed even their most careful planning. Still other times, I saw unscrupulous businesses that obscured loan terms or engaged in outright fraud.

Many people struggle to understand financial matters, and this lack of understanding can lead them into trouble or make their financial problems harder to overcome. At the CFPB, we are uniquely positioned to address these issues by helping to bridge the gap between people's actual financial capabilities and the increasingly complex financial decisions they have to make.

We are deeply committed to a vision of an America where everyone is financially educated. But the challenges that confront us in achieving this goal are complex, varied, and significant. To face these challenges, we must see that people can learn financial management skills throughout life – in schools and in places of work and worship. But we should start where all good education starts – with our children.

Young people today and future generations should not have to repeat the financial mistakes made by earlier generations. This is why the CFPB is supporting a plan to bring financial education into K-12 classrooms. We are also committed to engaging and supporting teachers and parents who are some of our most important allies. I believe the financial education policy recommendations outlined in this white paper have the potential to transform the financial lives of a generation of Americans.

We look forward to collaborating with the many public, private, and nonprofit stakeholders and allies to advance this policy dialogue and help bring meaningful financial education opportunities to millions of American youth.

Sincerely,
Richard Cordray

1. INTRODUCTION

The recent economic downturn raised awareness about the complex nature of our financial marketplace and how unprepared many Americans are to navigate the array of choices before them. The Dodd-Frank Wall Street Reform and Consumer Protection Act of 2010 established the Consumer Financial Protection Bureau (CFPB), and mandated the creation of the Office of Financial Education within the CFPB to educate American consumers and help them make better-informed financial decisions.

To prepare Americans to make sound financial decisions, the CFPB is pursuing a broad and holistic approach, which includes strategies that:

- Help make financial markets and products safer for consumers;
- Increase transparency to enable individuals to compare products and make informed decisions; and
- Promote policies that help consumers of all ages improve their financial knowledge and capability in ways that will enable them to navigate the financial marketplace effectively and take more control over their economic lives.

Consistent with this approach, the CFPB is also identifying opportunities for broader policy coordination on financial education among a range of stakeholders in the nonprofit, government, and private sectors.

The purpose of this white paper is to outline how the ongoing struggle of many consumers to manage their finances can be mitigated in the future by focusing specifically on youth financial education. What we propose here is a comprehensive strategy to impart personal financial-management skills to young people while they are in school. We are focusing on school-based financial education policy for two reasons: first, most Americans are poorly prepared to make informed financial decisions; second, school-based financial education has the potential to reverse the current trend of poor financial preparation for future generations of American consumers.

It is not difficult to understand why it is important for American consumers to master personal financial-management skills. American consumers often learn about managing their finances by making mistakes. Some of these mistakes can be very costly. For example, when consumers make an ordinary financial mistake such as being late on monthly credit card payments, they can have a poor credit report.

As we know, unfavorable credit reports can have potentially far-reaching consequences for consumers beyond the credit market. Organizations increasingly use credit reports to make decisions beyond determining a consumer's eligibility for credit. For example, organizations can access an individual's credit report when determining eligibility for rental housing and checking accounts, setting premiums for auto and casualty insurance in some states, and making hiring decisions. Consumers can trigger wide-ranging consequences when they make seemingly small mistakes. Thus, consumers need to acquire the knowledge, skills, and decision-making abilities to manage their finances.

From our vantage point, there is a very promising opportunity to help consumers become informed financial decision makers by focusing financial education efforts on young people. In the U.S., we should start young people on the road to continuous money management practice by systematically introducing age-appropriate financial education lessons and activities during the K-12 school years. When we start early with age-appropriate and relevant financial education and consistently reinforce those lessons throughout the K-12 years, we can give young people more chances to develop positive habits and behaviors.

Due to young people's current high levels of financial activity, it is imperative to introduce personal financial management early. America's children and youth spend roughly $211 billion annually.[1] According to the Financial Industry Regulatory Authority (FINRA) Investor Education Foundation's 2009 National Financial Capability Survey, approximately 72 percent of youth (defined as 18 to 24 years old) have a checking account and approximately 62 percent have a savings account, money-market account, or CD.[2]

Although young people tend to be unbanked or underbanked at higher rates than adults, they are increasingly utilizing a patchwork of newer financial products. Some of these products are offered by specialized providers through retail channels, including stored-value cards (e.g., gift cards), prepaid debit cards, while others are utilized online such as PayPal, and mobile payment methods. In light of these changes and the growing complexities of the marketplace, young people have a greater need than ever before for resources that help improve their financial knowledge and capability. Schools and youth centers are logical places to provide exposure to financial concepts and opportunities for practical experience.

As we further discuss our policy proposal, it is important to acknowledge that there is already an ongoing and well-developed conversation about promising practices in promoting financial education and capability for children and youth. The CFPB enters this conversation to facilitate a national focus on how state and local policy leaders can develop and implement comprehensive financial education strategies for K-12 students that are appropriate for their educational locales. Here, we briefly outline the five essential strategies that we believe could positively transform the financial lives of a generation of young Americans:

- **Recommendation 1:** Introduce key financial education concepts early and continue to build on that foundation consistently throughout the K-12 school years. In addition, CFPB encourages states to make a stand-alone financial education course a graduation requirement for high school students.
- **Recommendation 2:** Include personal financial management questions in standardized tests.
- **Recommendation 3:** Provide opportunities throughout the K-12 years to practice money management through innovative, hands-on learning opportunities.
- **Recommendation 4:** Create consistent opportunities and incentives for teachers to take financial education training with the express intention of teaching financial management to their students.
- **Recommendation 5:** Encourage parents and guardians to discuss money management topics at home and provide them with the tools necessary to have money conversations with their children.

The remainder of this white paper provides an overview of the financial decision-making context that Americans navigate, surveys some existing efforts in K-12 financial education, and addresses each of these elements of a comprehensive youth financial education strategy.

2. What Is the Problem?

This white paper identifies two main problems: First, many young people are ill-equipped to make major financial decisions, and second, young people confront a financial services marketplace that involves increasingly complex financial decisions.

Many young people transition to adulthood without having developed the basic financial knowledge, skills, and behaviors that are critical for establishing healthy financial futures. Many factors account for this, but chief among them are that 1) in most states, schools are not required to teach young people personal finance, and 2) many parents are unsure about when and how to talk to their children about money. As a result, young people have their first formal financial experiences when they enter the labor market lacking practical money management training or skills.

In addition to having their first financial experiences largely through their participation in the labor market, young people confront a financial marketplace that is significantly more complex than the one their parents first encountered as young adults. It is important to note that while earlier generations of Americans may only have had to choose among providers of savings and checking accounts and mortgage and auto lenders, today's youth have to choose from a large array of financial products and services. For example, in the payments arena, they may use prepaid debit cards, stored-value cards (e.g., gift cards), mobile methods of payments (such as "mobile carrier billing" where third parties can place charges on monthly phone bills, and/or online payment options such as PayPal). The array of choices now available to young consumers gives rise to a trend the Center for Financial Services Innovation (CFSI) labels an "a la carte" approach to financial services.[3]

Given the increasing complexity of the financial services landscape, young people have a greater need for resources to guide their financial decisions and improve their financial capability than may have been the case for earlier generations of Americans.[4]

Yet, the unfortunate fact is that young people are often unprepared to navigate this complex landscape. A 2008 national survey by the Jump$tart Coalition found that the "financial literacy of high school students has fallen to its lowest level ever, with a score of just 48.3 percent."[5] It appears that neither parents nor schools are adequately preparing students to manage their finances. A 2011 survey conducted by American Express found that a majority of parents with children in high school or college gave schools below-average or failing grades in teaching responsible spending.[6] Young people are vulnerable to misinformation and often make costly mistakes at important financial decision points.

The result of a poorly prepared youth population is a generation of consumers who struggle to make informed financial decisions. Indeed, a 2009 FINRA Investor Education Foundation survey of 28,000 American adults found that more than half of all respondents live paycheck-topaycheck and a significant majority of respondents (60 percent) reported not having a "rainy

day" fund to cover three months of unanticipated financial emergencies.[7] In addition, between 2004 and 2009, one in four respondents engaged in some form of high-cost, non-bank borrowing, including taking out a payday loan or getting an advance on a tax refund.[8] By failing to start young people on a path to successful personal money management, we leave a legacy of consumers who are ill-prepared to understand the risks and consequences of financial products, services, and decisions.

Young people are not prepared to manage their finances when they reach adulthood. At the same time, the current financial services marketplace is increasingly complex. In the face of this very real need, American education should include approaches to teach young people about their finances. Part of that task starts at home. But young people spend the majority of their time in school, therefore it makes sense to offer financial education early and consistently throughout the K-12 school years.

3. What Are the Current Approaches?

There is broad agreement on the importance of teaching financial education and capability to children and youth. However, there is little agreement about what constitutes effective financial education and capability initiatives. Thus, many organizations have developed a range of programs, and policies with varying state and national guidelines to help young people increase financial knowledge, develop money management skills, and in some cases, practice financial decision making.

The current landscape of programs geared toward improving the financial knowledge and capability of youth (e.g., access to appropriate products, skills, and decision-making) includes:

- Teaching financial education in K-12 schools;
- Providing "bank-at-school" programs;
- Providing matching incentives in specialized savings accounts;
- Providing non-school-based learning opportunities; and
- Using online learning tools and resources.

Many of these strategies and programs also employ experiential learning techniques.[9]

While there is a broad array of youth financial education strategies, there is, simultaneously, a relative absence of rigorous program evaluation and research to measure the effectiveness of existing financial education offerings. This makes it difficult for policymakers to determine which strategies to embrace and implement.[10]

In the following subsections, we review examples of K-12 financial education initiatives currently underway. These examples are illustrative of efforts occurring throughout the country. This discussion is not intended as an exhaustive overview of current programs, nor does it indicate an endorsement of these programs or the organizations associated with them.

3.1. Teaching Financial Education in Schools

A number of states have recognized the connection between including financial education into school curricula and financial capability later in life. As of 2011, policymakers in 22 states had enacted laws requiring high school students to take an economics course as a graduation requirement, and 13 states required students to take a personal finance course (or personal finance included in an economics course) as a high school graduation requirement.[11]

Popular approaches for teaching financial education in schools include the following:

- **Integrated curricula:** Adding financial education concepts and lessons into existing curricula enables students to see the intersection between core subjects (e.g., math, language arts, and social studies) and personal finance. For example, the K-6 *Everyday Math* program developed at the University of Chicago focuses on using math to solve practical problems (e.g., making change, doing tally lists), thereby getting financial issues into the standard mathematics curriculum.[12]
- **Separate curricula dedicated to teaching personal finance:** These classes are typically offered in high schools and are often geared toward graduating seniors who are on the verge of going out on their own as adults to become financially responsible for their own decisions. For example, Utah requires a stand-alone financial education course for high school graduation. Designed for juniors and seniors, the half-credit course teaches to four core standards: financial decision-making and goals; income and careers; principles of money management; and savings, investing, and retirement planning.

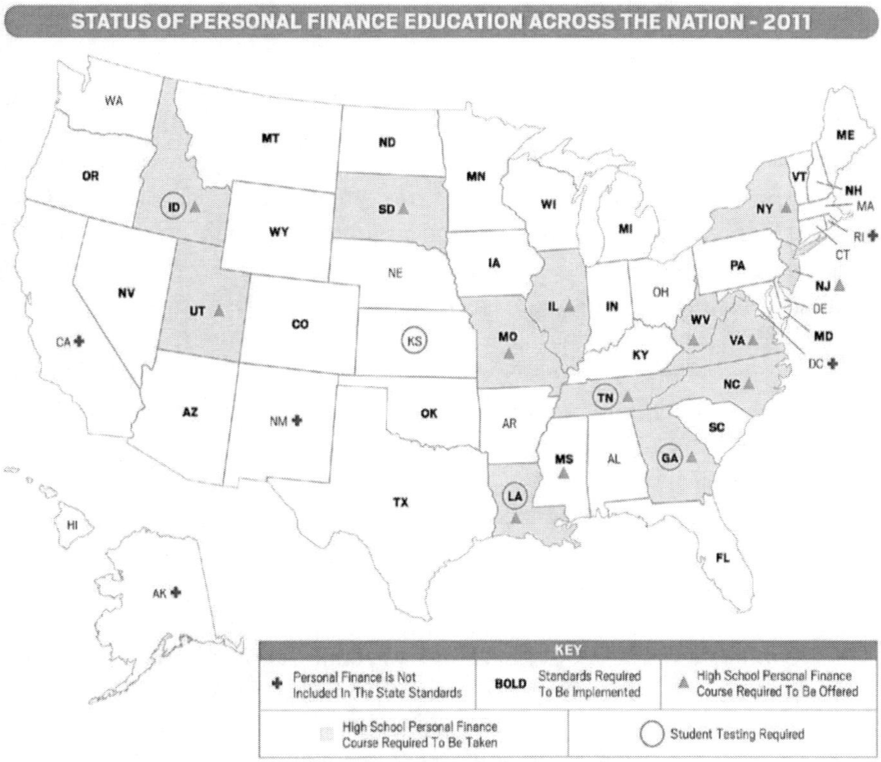

Source: Survey of the States, Council on Economic Education, http://www.councilforeconed.org/wp/wpcontent/uploads/2011/11/2011-Survey-of-the-States.pdf

Figure 1. Status of Personal Finance Education Across the Nation – 2011.

Many state and education leaders have also implemented education content standards for teaching personal finance. Education standards outline expectations about the knowledge, concepts, and skills that students should acquire at each grade level. Forty-six states now include personal finance in their curriculum standards.[13] It is important to note that states can adopt personal finance content standards but stop short of requiring schools to implement those standards. When the law does not require implementation of specific education standards, they become voluntary and less effective, tending to take a back seat to the required education standards.

3.2. Bank-at-School Programs

Schools throughout the country have partnered with banks and credit unions to start bank-at-school programs, which provide children and youth with classroom-based financial education, the opportunity to open deposit accounts on the school premises, and the ability to make regular small deposits. Many programs also give students the opportunity to manage the school bank or credit union branches as student bankers or junior tellers. Young students may learn more from financial education in classrooms when they can also practice using appropriate financial products and services. Students with savings accounts and the ability to make regular deposits at school have an opportunity to apply financial knowledge and skills learned in the classroom. This activity increases the relevance of the instruction and can lead to greater engagement.

Because many of the program designs and partnerships occur at the local or regional levels, it is unclear how many bank-at-school programs are in operation. Examples of such programs include:

- **School $ense and Money F-I-T:** School $ense is a bank-at-school program operating in Eau Clair, Wisconsin schools. The program provides personal finance instruction in fourth- and fifth-grade classes. In six of the 13 elementary schools in the Eau Clair school district, students have access to in-school credit union branches where students can open savings accounts and make regular savings deposits in these accounts. The Money F-I-T research pilot is examining whether fourth- and fifth-grade students learn more from personal finance instruction when they have a credit union branch in their school. The program will provide valuable insight into the effective strategies for teaching personal finance to elementary school students. A similar program, Smarter Texans Save, has been launched in Amarillo, Texas. As part of its Assessing Financial Capability Outcomes research initiative, the U.S. Department of the Treasury is funding the evaluation of the Money F-I-T research pilot.[14]
- **Capital One student-run bank branches:** Branches have been established in Newark, New Jersey, as well as in the Bronx and Harlem in New York City. The in-school branch offers a limited menu of products designed primarily for student savers. The school branch is managed by high school seniors who also teach fellow students the importance of money management skills.

- **Delaware Bank-at-School programs:** These programs give students access to savings accounts at no cost. As of 2012, the state had more than 70 bank-at-school sites with more than 4,000 depositors.[15] Students also have an opportunity to serve as junior tellers at the school branch. Although classroom financial education is not required, teachers receive financial education lessons that correlate with the state standards in economics.

3.3. Youth Savings Accounts

A number of organizations – particularly nonprofits, educational institutions, and government agencies – have developed savings accounts for children and youth with built-in matching incentives and/or prizes to promote the habit of saving, financial goal setting, and, in some programs, college access. These savings accounts are often paired with some form of financial education.

One positive correlation between having an account and having savings was documented in a 2010 study conducted by the Center for Social Development at Washington University in St. Louis, which found that students who expect to graduate from a four-year college and have an account are substantially more likely to attend college than youth who have no account.[16] Examples of savings products geared toward youth include:

- **Make Your Path (MY Path):** This initiative helps low-income youth in San Francisco develop healthy financial habits and behaviors by combining the following elements: financial education developed and delivered by peers; an emphasis on setting and achieving savings goals; opportunities to engage with common financial products and services such as savings accounts; and a focus on behavioral economics that removes barriers to account setup through automated savings-account setup. The pilot uses a hands-on, experiential approach, with an emphasis on peer learning and support. Mission SF Community Financial Center launched this program in 2011 in partnership with the Mayor's Youth Employment and Education Program, the city's largest youth employment program.
- **Kindergarten to College (K2C):** The first publicly-funded, universal children's college savings-account program in the U.S., this program provides every kindergartener attending public school in San

Francisco with a college savings account containing a $50 deposit from the city and county of San Francisco. Children enrolled in the National Student Lunch Program receive an additional $50 deposit. The program offers incentives to save earlier and to save more. Foundations, community organizations, local businesses, and individuals provide additional deposits and matching incentives. In addition, schools are integrating financial subjects into the K-12 math curriculum, with each child's K2C account serving as a teaching tool.

- **Youth Savings Account:** This program gives Native American high school students in two participating New Mexico schools access to a savings account and a $50 seed deposit. Students who keep the account open and make deposits are entered into a lottery to win $100 at the end of the semester. This program pairs access to incentivized savings accounts with classroom financial education. The program is offered by First Nations Development Institute.
- **KIPP College Account:** This special savings account is available to students in grades five through 12 at some KIPP DC schools. The account provides a $50 seed deposit and additional dollar-for-dollar matching incentives. Students who go on to college receive the accumulated savings in the form of a scholarship.

3.4. Non-School-Based Learning

Many financial education courses are conducted via community programs and services. This helps take some pressure off schools dealing with funding challenges and allows for other funding opportunities. Faith-based groups, community organizations, industry trade associations, and others are creating opportunities to provide financial education to youth. By offering tailored programs, materials, and other avenues of learning accessible to students, these groups help youth who may otherwise not have an opportunity to be exposed to financial education. Examples of these programs include:

- **Junior Achievement Finance Park:** This program helps students build financial skills by engaging them in experiential, hands-on learning opportunities on topics related to entrepreneurship, work readiness, and financial literacy. The on-site activities are managed in a dynamic environment outside the classroom. There are 15 permanent Junior Achievement Finance Park facilities across the country.

- **The Boys and Girls Clubs of America:** In collaboration with the Charles Schwab Foundation, the Boys and Girls Clubs of America educate teens about money and finance through the Money Matters: Make It Count Program.[17] This financial literacy program consists of interactive activities and exercises on topics such as using a checking account, creating a spending plan, managing debt, saving for college, and learning the basics of investing.
- **National Endowment for Financial Education (NEFE):** This program emphasizes the importance of using multiple financial-literacy tools to educate young people. Fun online games, classroom instruction, community-based learning, and home-based study can all work toward producing well-rounded, highly-efficient, financially-literate students. The NEFE High School Financial Planning Program provides students in grades eight through 12 with the opportunity to develop personal-finance skills.
- **4-H Youth Development:** This program offers a variety of age-appropriate, financial-learning experiences for youth ranging from Reading Makes Cents to 4-H Build a Million. The 4-H program's learn-by-doing philosophy engages youth in strategies to learn financial terms and practice financial activities, including being treasurers of their 4-H clubs. As they learn how to budget and manage their projects from start to finish, they develop lifelong financial capability.[18]

3.5. Online Teaching Tools and Resources

The financial education field has developed an array of online teaching tools for supporting financial education. Examples of the types of offerings available include online training modules, online or mobile gaming (also known as financial entertainment), as well as numerous websites with useful calculators and resources.

- **MyMoney.Gov:** The website organizes financial education resources from more than 20 different federal agencies and websites in one place. This federal government website is dedicated to helping all Americans learn the basics of financial education. The website provides information, tools, and resources to help consumers make sound financial choices.

- **Money Smart Young Adult:** The Federal Deposit Insurance Corporation offers this program. This free, self-paced program for youths 13 and older features a game-based learning design. In addition, the program aligns with educational standards in all 50 states, the District of Columbia, Guam, and the Virgin Islands, as well as Jump$tart financial education standards and the economic education standards developed by the National Council on Economic Education.
- **Practical Money Skills for Life:** Developed by Visa, this website allows consumers, educators, parents, students, and policymakers to access free financial education resources, such as a pre-K-12 curriculum; online games (such as financial football); and videos developed in partnership with Khan Academy, a nonprofit that provides original lessons on a range of subjects through free video content.
- **Doorways to Dreams (D2D):** This national nonprofit has created games to improve financial engagement and capability of low-and moderate-income (LMI) consumers. Although these financial-entertainment games are geared toward women and LMI adults, player data revealed that the games were growing organically in popularity among high schoolers and middle schoolers. Through partnerships with government and education leaders, D2D hosts tournaments where youth play the games for the chance to win prizes such as $25 savings accounts and scholarships.
- **Vault – Understand Money and EverFi – Financial Literacy:** These learning platforms use video, animation, 3-D gaming, avatars, and social networking to bring complex financial concepts to life for children and youth. Vault – Understanding Money is an interactive program designed to teach and help students in grades four through six build the foundation for making good financial decisions. EverFi – Financial Literacy is a new-media program geared at students in grades nine through 12 that covers topics such as credit cards, savings, and investments.

3.6. Additional Experiential Learning Opportunities

Experiential learning is an important way to increase student engagement and improve learning. Experiential learning involves a cycle of action, reflection, conceptualization, and new experiences.[19] Teaching methods in experiential education include practice-based learning, role-play, simulation, imagination, inner exploration, encounter, and group work. A number of programs and strategies that have already been highlighted, at their core, provide opportunities to learn through experiential techniques. For example, programs that pair financial education with savings accounts at schools, special goal-based savings accounts with built-in incentives, and game-based learning all have some element of experiential learning. Additional examples of experiential learning opportunities include:

- **Girl Scouts of the USA:** This organization provides young girls with money-earning projects such as selling cookies. As part of this program, girls learn about goal setting, decision-making, and money management, among other things. This program employs encounter-based experiential learning to help girls gain financial knowledge and develop important skills. In 2011, Girl Scouts of the USA introduced a new set of financial-literacy badges for girls in K-12 grades.
- **Boys Scouts of America:** The Boy Scouts offer a merit badge for personal management. Earning the badge means the Boy Scout set short- and long-term financial goals and discussed them with his family; developed a spending plan; balanced a budget; put money into a savings account; analyzed how to manage money better; and studied insurance, cost of credit, and how to manage debt, as well as investing in stocks, bonds, and mutual funds.[20]
- **My Classroom Economy:** This classroom-management system is available to K-12 educators to teach age-appropriate personal-finance lessons through experiential learning. Teachers and students establish a simple classroom economic system where students need to earn a paycheck in the form of "school dollars" by taking on classroom jobs. With the school dollars they earn, students are required to pay rent for their desks, pay fines for violations, and have the option to invest with accumulated savings. This program helps students learn financial skills and decision-making through simulations and role-playing.

4. CFPB's Recommendations for Advancing Financial Education and Capability

States can help determine the quantity and quality of the financial education that most students receive through a variety of policy options. States can explicitly mandate that high school students complete a stand-alone course in personal finance. In addition, states can require school districts to include personal finance in the curriculum of other courses, such as family and consumer sciences, economics, mathematics, business education, agricultural sciences, and social studies. As an incremental step, states can require schools to offer an elective course in personal finance, but stop short of making it a condition for graduation.[21] This plurality of policy solutions adopted by states reinforces the broad agreement that it is good public policy to include financial education in the K-12 curriculum.

Because education policy is determined at the state and local levels, there is a range of approaches for supporting financial education. This raises the question of whether more can be done to pursue a common policy framework that supports the current diverse approaches among states. While there can and should be many types of financial education in schools – particularly to reflect the unique needs and diversity of each community – these approaches could benefit from sharing a common strategic point of departure. In this respect, the development of the Common Core State Standards is instructive. Forty-five states, the District of Columbia, four territories, and the Department of Defense Education Activity have adopted the Common Core Standards in K-12 Mathematics and English Language Arts.[22] These new standards create a shared understanding of the cognitive theory behind the organization, approach, and curricula for Math and English Language Arts.

A coordinated strategy similar to the Common Core could anchor the efforts underway to provide financial education and capability in schools. In our view, there is sufficient directional evidence to propose a comprehensive strategic policy framework for financial education in schools; the evidence will be discussed below.

We believe that these five essential strategies, if implemented by state policymakers and education leaders, could transform the financial lives of a generation of young Americans:

- **Recommendation 1:** Introduce key financial education concepts early and continue to build on that foundation consistently throughout the

K-12 school years. In addition, CFPB encourages states to make a stand-alone financial education course a graduation requirement for high school students.

- **Recommendation 2:** Include personal financial management questions in standardized tests.
- **Recommendation 3:** Provide opportunities throughout the K-12 years to practice money management through innovative, hands-on learning opportunities.
- **Recommendation 4:** Create consistent opportunities and incentives for teachers to take financial education training with the express intention of teaching financial management to their students.
- **Recommendation 5:** Encourage parents and guardians to discuss money management topics at home and provide them with the tools necessary to have money conversations with their children.

4.1. Teach Financial Education Early and Consistently through K-12 Years

Most U.S. students spend an average of six-and-a-half hours per day in school for 180 days a year.[23] By the time they graduate, we expect them to be able to read, write, master everyday math skills, engage in effective teamwork, and possess some personal judgment that helps them make sound decisions. When young people transition to adulthood, they also confront a number of financial decisions: how to use credit, how to manage household expenses with earnings, and what types of financial products to use. Yet, in a number of states financial education is absent from the school day throughout the 13 years that students spend in the K-12 realm.

When young people lack the skills to engage in effective financial decision-making, they can incur unnecessary debt, miss opportunities to save money, and develop a poor credit history. The absence of money management skills can have a significant impact on their ability to access basic necessities, such as checking and savings accounts, rental housing, and employment – opportunities and resources that are essential to building financial stability. It is unfortunate that such critical life skills are often left out of the required course of study.

Why is it important to focus on building these financial skills early? First, when we teach financial concepts early, we can catch young people at critical developmental stages and can influence how they manage financial matters throughout their lives. Cognitive development theory and related research suggests that the elementary school years may be a window of opportunity during which education can influence financial behavior later in life.[24] Although young children's financial understanding is unsophisticated, scholars suggest that elementary school-age children can grasp basic economic concepts such as savings, barter, scarcity, and supply and demand.[25] Second, recent research demonstrates that young people begin to form financial identities early and that those identities are correlated with financial capability later in life.[26] It is clear that starting financial education early has important benefits for young people.

In addition to starting early, youth financial education should be continuous. Like other areas of study, developing financial knowledge, skills, and the decision-making capacity needed to navigate the financial services marketplace successfully requires consistent learning opportunities throughout a person's education and even throughout a person's lifetime. By integrating financial education lessons in school curricula – such as the Family, Career and Community Leaders of America programs led by Family and Consumer Sciences educators – students can learn, for instance, about the benefits of compound interest in math class, the basics of economic costs and risks in social studies class, and sharpen writing skills by composing essays about how we manage money or how we can take control of our financial lives to achieve our goals.

When we start early and build financial skills throughout their K-12 education, we give young people time to grow and comprehend more as they go through natural developmental stages.[27] A longitudinal research study of university students conducted in 2011 as part of the Arizona Pathways for Life Success in University Students (APLUS) program found that high school and college students who are exposed to ongoing or cumulative financial education show an increase in financial knowledge, which, in turn, drives increasingly responsible financial behavior as they become young adults.[28] This opportunity to find this "teachable moment" as young people transition to adulthood is the key reason why state and education leaders should strongly consider adoption of a required stand-alone course in personal finance for high school students. Indeed, a 2009 study revealed that college students from states that require a financial education course had the highest reported financial knowledge and were more likely to display positive financial behaviors and dispositions.[29]

Although we need more research and data to inform specific program and curricula design, there is some evidence to suggest that teaching financial concepts early and consistently increases financial capability.

4.2. Introduce Financial Education Concepts into Standardized Tests

Forty-five states, four U.S. territories, the District of Columbia, and the Department of Defense Educational Activity have all adopted the Common Core State Standards.[30] There is a unique opportunity for this group of states and jurisdictions to incorporate financial education questions in standardized assessments. The benefit of doing so is that schools and teachers will have added incentives to teach to topics queried in those assessments. In addition, this presents an opportunity to systematically measure and track the performance of students on financial education content.

Since financial education is not part of the Common Core State Standards, it will likely not figure prominently in curricula the states adopt. This raises the possibility that financial education concepts might not be included in standardized assessments unless they are incorporated into an existing educational standard in Math or English Language Arts. In 2002, the Treasury Department suggested that states explicitly develop policy principles that affirm a state's commitment to teaching financial skills and require that financial education concepts get included in test questions. Under this approach, when a state issues a Request for Proposal to develop educational assessments, the companies bidding for those state contracts would have strong incentives to incorporate financial education into the tests they propose and ultimately develop.[31]

The CFPB urges states to explore opportunities to support the development of assessment questions related to financial skills. In states where the Common Core Standards have been adopted, state and education leaders should consider aligning financial skills based assessment questions with the existing standards. If such assessment questions are developed for one state, it is likely that other states that work within the Common Core framework can use that states work as a reference point in developing their own assessments for financial education.

What would a standardized assessment question about financial education concepts look like? In a 2010 *Chronicle of Higher Education* article, Professor Peter Tufano of Harvard University suggested that it would not require adding more content-based questions, but rather reframing the context of existing questions.

> For example, in the critical-reading section of the SAT, test takers are given passages... and asked what they mean. Those passages could be about credit cards, or insurance. In the math section, students solve word problems. Reframing some questions around key financial principles, such as interest compounding, would be straightforward.
>
> Testing services already have experience with this material, which is included in the GMAT, taken by M.B.A. applicants.[32]

The Doorways to Dreams Fund, a nonprofit organization founded by Professor Tufano provides an excellent example of a sample math question that could be incorporated into standardized exams required for college admission.

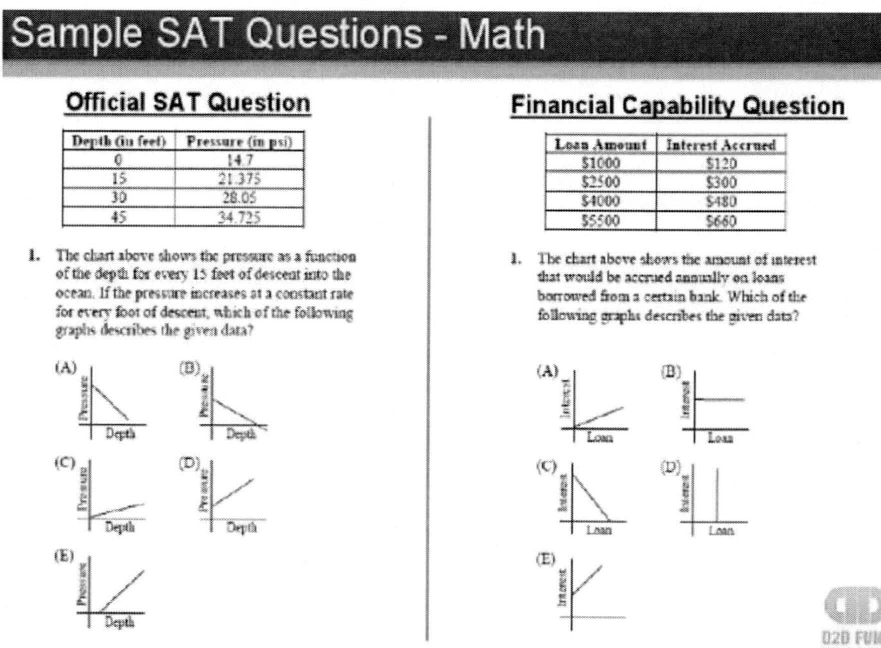

Source: Prep for Change Overview, D2D Fund, http://www.d2dfund.org/prep change 1

Figure 2. Sample Standardized Exam questions for Math.

4.3. Create Innovative Hands-on Learning Opportunities

Experiential learning is the process whereby students "learn by doing" and by reflecting on the experience. Students may be more likely to retain financial knowledge when they apply the concepts they have learned in concrete situations.[33] Examples of hands-on learning opportunities for children and youth include interacting with financial products and services, either through simulations or through in-school bank and credit union branches; online gaming to gain financial knowledge and practice financial decision-making skills; and entrepreneurship training.

Programs that incorporate access to financial services may increase the effectiveness of financial education curricula.[34] Several leaders in the education field have developed hands-on financial education opportunities for youth. Many of these programs are based on the belief that financial education that is relevant to students and provides experiential learning opportunities may be more effective in motivating learning and improving retention.

Some promising examples of hands-on learning programs for K-12 students are Kindergarten To College (K2C) and Make Your Path (MY Path). A case study of the K2C program conducted by EARN showed that parents participating in the universal college savings program found flexible account features very appealing (82 percent), consider teachers and school principals to be the best messengers of the program (71 percent and 65 percent, respectively), and believe that financial education in the classroom for students and community programs for parents is very appealing or somewhat appealing (52 percent and 36 percent, respectively).[35]

An initial evaluation of the MY Path program was conducted by the Federal Reserve Bank of San Francisco. The research revealed that low-income youth participating in the MY Path program demonstrated in pre- and post-test assessments that they had significantly increased their knowledge of various financial topics after each peer-led financial education training session.[36] Participants also reported that they increased their frequency of positive financial behaviors as a result of the program (e.g., budgeting, tracking spending, distinguishing between needs and wants, etc.).[37] Individuals also indicated that participating in peer-led financial education training increased the level of engagement in part because they were able to relate better to the youth trainers.[38]

Many of the innovative hands-on learning programs that have been developed are too new to suggest robust results at the moment. Yet the interim results discussed in this section suggest that these trials are having a positive impact on the financial knowledge and outlook of children and youth. Our knowledge of what can be successful in transferring personal financial management skills to young people will be enhanced by extensive exploration and evaluation of learning-by-doing opportunities.

4.4. Create Consistent Opportunities and Incentives for Teacher Training

Teachers are critical to the success of any programs or initiatives that rely on teaching financial education in classrooms. A growing body of research suggests that teachers generally support financial education course requirements for students. A 2010 teacher survey funded by the National Endowment for Financial Education found that 89 percent of K-12 teachers agree that students should either take a financial education course or pass a competency test for high school graduation. In the same survey, only 20 percent of teachers, however, believe that they are adequately prepared to teach personal finance topics.[39]

Teachers confront continuing education obstacles that include having limited or uneven access to trainings and few incentives for participating in training programs that will help them become better educators of personal finance. Barriers to accessing teacher training are especially acute for educators in geographically remote areas because they are forced into costly, long-distance travel to attend training. Connecting teachers to existing resources, increasing access to training by offering continuing-education units (CEUs), and providing need-based stipends for teachers who must travel to attend trainings could remove some initial barriers for educators.

There are many demands on teachers to get training in specific content areas, and they also have an array of training options that provide CEUs and compete with financial education training. One way to address this challenge is to develop a systematic approach to awarding CEUs to all teachers who avail themselves of ongoing financial education training programs. States and school districts should consider this policy recommendation to ensure consistent opportunities for teachers across the country. We can also think about how to integrate personal financial management training into college courses for those considering becoming teachers. If colleges and universities offer effective financial education courses, these courses could have special value for education students who will later become teachers.

If teachers have better access to high-quality training for teaching financial education – combined with the incentive of CEUs – more American students are likely to receive and benefit from financial education lessons taught in K-12 classrooms.

4.5. Encourage Parents to Discuss Money Management Topics at Home

As common sense would suggest, parents influence children's habits, attitudes, and even financial capability. A longitudinal research study found that not only do parents exert the most influence over their children when it comes to developing positive financial attitudes and behaviors, but they are also 1.5 times more influential than ongoing financial education.[40] Similarly, research in the field of identity development and developmental psychology has found that parents are very influential in shaping consumer skills and knowledge as well.[41] Evidence suggests that as youth enter adulthood, parents continue to influence children's financial behaviors and skills. Working with parents to encourage and support money conversations at home is critical to putting young people on the path to exercising greater control over their personal finances.

This evidence suggests an enormous and exciting opportunity to engage parents and guardians in their children's financial education. There are many ways we can accomplish such engagement, in ways that are similar to how parents become active in supporting their children's extracurricular activities, academic projects, and general learning and skill acquisition.

While parents and family members are important transmitters of lessons about how a young person should approach personal financial management, many parents, like teachers, may lack knowledge and skills in this area. As the 2009 National Financial Capability Study indicates, many Americans possess a low level of financial literacy as measured by quiz-style questions designed to yield an independent, objective assessment of the respondent's financial literacy.[42] Parents need educational tools and opportunities to support lessons on money management that their children may be learning in school.

CONCLUSION

Financial capability is critical to the success and achievement of Americans. We know that at a relatively early age, young people face challenging and life-changing financial decisions. Yet many Americans lack the personal financial management skills to be successful. This white paper focuses on how we can address the absence of personal financial management skills by focusing on opportunities to engage young people during their K-12 years.

Across the country, policymakers, teachers, nonprofit leaders, and parents are pursuing a wide range of approaches for teaching financial education and capability. Notwithstanding these efforts, there is an exciting opportunity to develop a coordinated and consistent policy framework that can provide young people with the information, experience, and results they need to be informed and empowered managers of their money over their lifetimes.

The policy framework articulated in this white paper acknowledges the importance of starting early to support financial capability and continuing this emphasis throughout the K-12 school years. In addition, CFPB recommends that states strongly consider including a stand-alone personal financial management course as a graduation requirement for high school students. It also advocates that financial management questions be added to standardized assessments. The policy framework includes an emphasis on financial education approaches that offers opportunities for experiential learning so students are able to apply financial knowledge in concrete ways and build financial capability. A number of states, municipalities, and school districts have engaged in pilot initiatives that provide young people with hands-on experiences that will yield important lessons for the field and will facilitate effective future efforts.

A number of states require financial education and some require financial education testing. The CFPB recommends that states consider removing teacher training barriers and award teachers CEUs for pursuing ongoing training to teach financial skills effectively. Finally, we propose that schools engage with parents to develop strategies for supporting the financial capability of young people.

In order to navigate the complex financial marketplace, consumers need to be able to discern the risks as well as the opportunities associated with financial products, services, and decisions. Young people today and future generations should not have to repeat the financial mistakes made by earlier generations.

Our financial education policy recommendations outlined in this white paper represent a comprehensive approach to addressing the complex and dynamic issue of promoting the financial education and capability of millions of young Americans. If implemented by state policy makers and education leaders, these recommendations have the potential to help transform the financial lives of a generation of children and youth. These policy recommendations are self-reinforcing and could create a stronger policy fabric if they are pursued together rather than independently.

End Notes

[1] 2012 Harris Poll Youth Plus. Harris Interactive. "$211 Billion and So Much to Buy – American Youths, the New Big Spenders." http://www.harrisinteractive.com/NewsRoom/PressReleases/tabid/446/ctl/ReadCustom%20Default/mid/1506/ArticleId/896/Default.aspx (October 26, 2011) (accessed April 5, 2013).

[2] FINRA Investor Education Foundation. "Financial Capability in the United States, 2009 Nation Financial Capability Study." http://www.finrafoundation.org/web/groups/foundation/@foundation/documents/foundation/p120535.pdf (accessed April 1, 2013): 51-52.

[3] Stone, Corey, and Joshua Sledge. "Financial First Encounters: The Fractured Financial Landscape Facing Youth Today." http://www.cfsinnovation.com/publications/article/440710 (accessed April 4, 2013): 5.

[4] Stone, Corey, and Joshua Sledge. "Financial First Encounters: The Fractured Financial Landscape Facing Youth Today." http://www.cfsinnovation.com/publications/article/440710 (accessed April 4, 2013): 5.

[5] Mandell, Lewis. "The Financial Literacy of Young American Adults: Results of the 2008 National Jump$tart Coalition Survey of High School Seniors and College Students." http://www.jumpstart.org/assets/files/2008SurveyBook.pdf (accessed April 4, 2013) (2008): 5.

[6] American Express. "No Triple 'AAA' Ratings for Schools That Fail to Teach 'Safe Spend.'" http://about.americanexpress.com/news/pr/2011/safespend.aspx (accessed April 8, 2013) (August 10, 2011).

[7] FINRA Investor Education Foundation. "States Ranked Most and Least Likely to Engage in Five Key Measures of Financial Capability, 2009 National Financial Capability Study." http://www.usfinancialcapability.org/download/State_rankings_rev_101202.pdf (accessed April 12, 2013).

[8] FINRA Investor Education Foundation. "States Ranked Most and Least Likely to Engage in Five Key Measures of Financial Capability, 2009 National Financial Capability Study." http://www.usfinancialcapability.org/download/State_rankings_rev_101202.pdf (accessed April 12, 2013).

[9] Experiential learning is the process of deriving meaning from direct or hands-on experiences.

[10] Although the Center for Financial Services Innovation has provided some guidance by identifying those program elements that have been found to be effective at promoting financial capability, it is clear that additional, rigorously derived evidence and data would be required for policymakers to choose among those financial education curricula and

programs that consistently promote behavioral change and positive financial outcomes later in life. Center for Financial Services Innovation. "From Financial Education to Financial Capability: Opportunities for Innovation." http://www.cfsinnovation.com/system/files/InBrief_FinancialCapability_Mar22010.pdf (accessed April 12, 2013).

[11] Council on Economic Education, "Survey of the States," http://www.councilforeconed.org/wp/wpcontent/uploads/2011/11/2011-Survey-of-the-States.pdf (March 2012) (accessed April 20, 2013): 7.

[12] University of Chicago School Mathematics Project, Everyday Mathematics, http://everydaymath.uchicago.edu/about/, (accessed April 20,2013)

[13] CFED: Assets & Opportunity Scorecard. "Policy Brief: Financial Education in Schools." http://cfed.org/assets/scorecard/2013/pbFinancialEducationSchools2013.pdf (October 2012) (accessed April 5, 2013).

[14] Money F-I-T, Center for Financial Security, accessed April 23, 2013, http://moneyfitcfs.com/aboutmoney-f-i-t/ ,

[15] Delaware Financial Literacy Institute website. http://www.dfli.org/index.cfm?ref=05000 (accessed April 4, 2013).

[16] Elliott III, William, and Sondra Beverly. "The Role of Savings and Wealth in Reducing 'Wilt' Between Expectations and College Attendance." *Journal of Children & Poverty,* 17 (2) (2011): 165.

[17] Money Matters: Make It Count. Program information. http://moneymattersmakeitcount.com/Pages/default.aspx (accessed April 8, 2013).

[18] 4-H Youth Development. Ohio State University Extension. *Real Money. Real World.* http://realmoneyrealworld.osu.edu/documents/RMRWFollowUpStudyexecsum.pdf (2009): 2.

[19] Johnson, Elizabeth and Margaret S. Sherraden. "From Financial Literacy to Financial Capability Among Youth." Working Paper 06-11 (2006) (accessed April 8, 2013):11.

[20] Boy Scouts of America. Personal Management Merit Badge Series (BSA Supply No. 35928). http://www.scouting.org/scoutsource/BoyScouts/AdvancementandAwards/MeritBadges/mb-PERM.aspx (accessed April 11, 2013).

[21] By making financial education optional, however, many students are able to graduate without developing important financial skills.

[22] In the States. Common Core State Standards Initiative. http://www.corestandards.org/in-the-states (accessed April 12, 2013).

[23] The Center for Public Education. "Time in School: How Does the U.S. Compare?" http://www.centerforpubliceducation.org/Main-Menu/Organizing-a-school/Time-in-school-How-does-the-UScompare (accessed April 5, 2013).

[24] Collins, J. Michael et al. "Determining What Works: A Framework for Evaluating Financial Literacy Education in Elementary School." Center for Financial Security. http://moneyfitevaluation.files.wordpress.com/2012/06/determining-what-works-2012.pdf (accessed April 1, 2013): 3.

[25] Sherraden, Margaret S., Lissa Johnson, Baorong Guo, and William Elliott. "Financial Capability in Children: Effects of Participation in a School-Based Financial Education and Savings Program." *Journal of Family and Economic Issues.* 32 (3) (2011): 385-399.

[26] Shim, Soyeon, Joyce Serido, Leslie Bosch, and Chuanyi Tang. "Financial Identity Processing Styles Among Young Adults." *The Journal of Consumer Affairs* (Spring 2013): 128-152.

[27] Lopez-Fernandini, Alejandra and Karen Murrell. "The Effectiveness of Youth Financial Education." New America Foundation. http://www.newamerica.net/publications/policy/effectivenessyouthfinancialeducation1 (accessed March 29, 2013).

[28] Shim, Soyeon, and Joyce Serido. "Young Adults' Financial Capability." APLUS, Wave 2. http://www.cgsnet.org/ckfinder/userfiles/files/APLUSWave2Final.pdf (September 2011) (accessed April 4, 2013): 16.

[29] Gutter, Michael. "Financial Management Practices of College Students from States with Varying Financial Education Mandates." National Endowment for Financial Education. http://www.nefe.org/Portals/0/WhatWeProvide/PrimaryResearch/PDF/Gutter FinMgtPracticesofCollegeStudents Final.pdf (2009) (accessed April 8, 2013).

[30] In the States. Common Core State Standards Initiative. http://www.corestandards.org/in-the-states (accessed April 12, 2013).

[31] U.S. Department of the Treasury, Office of Financial Education (white paper). "Integrating Financial Education Into School Curricula: Giving America's Youth the Educational Foundation for Making Effective Financial Decisions Throughout Their Lives by Teaching Financial Concepts as Part of Math and Reading Curricula in Elementary, Middle, and High Schools." http://www.eric.ed.gov/PDFS/ED471873.pdf (October 2002) (accessed April 8, 2013).

[32] Tufano, Peter. "Commentary: Leveraging Admissions Tests to Increase Financial Savvy." *Chronicle of Higher Education.* http://chronicle.com/article/Leveraging-Admissions-Tests-to/125177/ (October 31, 2010) (accessed April 8, 2013).

[33] Collins, J. Michael et al. "Determining What Works: A Framework for Evaluating Financial Literacy Education in Elementary School." Center for Financial Security. http://moneyfitevaluation.files.wordpress.com/2012/06/determining-what-works-2012.pdf (accessed April 1, 2013): 11.

[34] Peng, Tzu-Chin Martina, Suzanne Bartholomae, Jonathan Fox, and Garrett Cravener. "The Impact of Personal Finance Delivered in High School and College Courses." *Journal of Family and Economic Issues,* 28(2) (2007): 265- 284.

[35] Shipman Bevans, Jade. "Children's Education Savings Accounts: A Case Study of San Francisco's Kindergarten to College Program." http://www.earn.org/static/uploads/files /K2C_ Practitioners_Report_.pdf (March 2013) (accessed April 8, 2013).

[36] Federal Reserve Bank of San Francisco. "Increasing Financial Capability Among Economically Vulnerable Youth: MY Path." http://www.frbsf.org/publications/community /wpapers/2013/working_paper_2013_03_IncreasingFinancial-Capability-among-Economically-Vulnerable-Youth-MY-Path.html (March 2013) (accessed April 8, 2013): 10.

[37] Federal Reserve Bank of San Francisco. "Increasing Financial Capability Among Economically Vulnerable Youth: MY Path." http://www.frbsf.org/publications/community /wpapers/2013/working_paper_2013_03_IncreasingFinancial-Capability-among-Economically-Vulnerable-Youth-MY-Path.html (March 2013) (accessed April 8, 2013): 11.

[38] Federal Reserve Bank of San Francisco. "Increasing Financial Capability Among Economically Vulnerable Youth: MY Path." http://www.frbsf.org/publications/community /wpapers/2013/working_paper_2013_03_IncreasingFinancial-Capability-among-Economically-Vulnerable-Youth-MY-Path.html (March 2013) (accessed April 8, 2013): 13.

[39] Way, Wendy L. and Karen Holden. "Teachers' Background & Capacity to Teach Personal Finance: Results of a National Study." National Endowment for Financial Education. http://www.nefe.org/Portals/0/WhatWeProvide/PrimaryResearch/PDF/TNTSalon_Executiv eSummary.pdf (accessed March 29, 2013): 13.

[40] Shim, Soyeon and Joyce Serido. "Young Adults' Financial Capability." APLUS, Wave 2. http://www.nefe.org/Portals/0/WhatWeProvide/PrimaryResearch/PDF/APLUSWave2_Final .pdf (September 2011) (accessed April 8, 2013): 21.

[41] Shim, Soyeon, Joyce Serido, Leslie Bosch, and Chuanyi Tang. "Financial Identity Processing Styles Among Young Adults." *The Journal of Consumer Affairs*, (Spring 2013): 131-148.

[42] FINRA Investor Education Foundation. "Financial Capability in the United States, 2009 Nation Financial Capability Study." http://www.finrafoundation.org/web/groups/foundation/@foundation/documents/foundation/p120535.pdf (accessed April 1, 2013): 18.

INDEX

U

V

W

Y